C-3339   CAREER EXAMINATION SERIES

This is your
PASSBOOK for...

Data Entry Clerk

Test Preparation Study Guide
Questions & Answers

COPYRIGHT NOTICE

This book is SOLELY intended for, is sold ONLY to, and its use is RESTRICTED to individual, bona fide applicants or candidates who qualify by virtue of having seriously filed applications for appropriate license, certificate, professional and/or promotional advancement, higher school matriculation, scholarship, or other legitimate requirements of education and/or governmental authorities.

This book is NOT intended for use, class instruction, tutoring, training, duplication, copying, reprinting, excerption, or adaptation, etc., by:

1) Other publishers
2) Proprietors and/or Instructors of "Coaching" and/or Preparatory Courses
3) Personnel and/or Training Divisions of commercial, industrial, and governmental organizations
4) Schools, colleges, or universities and/or their departments and staffs, including teachers and other personnel
5) Testing Agencies or Bureaus
6) Study groups which seek by the purchase of a single volume to copy and/or duplicate and/or adapt this material for use by the group as a whole without having purchased individual volumes for each of the members of the group
7) Et al.

Such persons would be in violation of appropriate Federal and State statutes.

PROVISION OF LICENSING AGREEMENTS – Recognized educational, commercial, industrial, and governmental institutions and organizations, and others legitimately engaged in educational pursuits, including training, testing, and measurement activities, may address request for a licensing agreement to the copyright owners, who will determine whether, and under what conditions, including fees and charges, the materials in this book may be used them. In other words, a licensing facility exists for the legitimate use of the material in this book on other than an individual basis. However, it is asseverated and affirmed here that the material in this book CANNOT be used without the receipt of the express permission of such a licensing agreement from the Publishers. Inquiries re licensing should be addressed to the company, attention rights and permissions department.

All rights reserved, including the right of reproduction in whole or in part, in any form or by any means, electronic or mechanical, including photocopying, recording, or by any information storage and retrieval system, without permission in writing from the Publisher.

Copyright © 2024 by
National Learning Corporation

212 Michael Drive, Syosset, NY 11791
(516) 921-8888 • www.passbooks.com
E-mail: info@passbooks.com

PASSBOOK® SERIES

THE *PASSBOOK® SERIES* has been created to prepare applicants and candidates for the ultimate academic battlefield – the examination room.

At some time in our lives, each and every one of us may be required to take an examination – for validation, matriculation, admission, qualification, registration, certification, or licensure.

Based on the assumption that every applicant or candidate has met the basic formal educational standards, has taken the required number of courses, and read the necessary texts, the *PASSBOOK® SERIES* furnishes the one special preparation which may assure passing with confidence, instead of failing with insecurity. Examination questions – together with answers – are furnished as the basic vehicle for study so that the mysteries of the examination and its compounding difficulties may be eliminated or diminished by a sure method.

This book is meant to help you pass your examination provided that you qualify and are serious in your objective.

The entire field is reviewed through the huge store of content information which is succinctly presented through a provocative and challenging approach – the question-and-answer method.

A climate of success is established by furnishing the correct answers at the end of each test.

You soon learn to recognize types of questions, forms of questions, and patterns of questioning. You may even begin to anticipate expected outcomes.

You perceive that many questions are repeated or adapted so that you can gain acute insights, which may enable you to score many sure points.

You learn how to confront new questions, or types of questions, and to attack them confidently and work out the correct answers.

You note objectives and emphases, and recognize pitfalls and dangers, so that you may make positive educational adjustments.

Moreover, you are kept fully informed in relation to new concepts, methods, practices, and directions in the field.

You discover that you are actually taking the examination all the time: you are preparing for the examination by "taking" an examination, not by reading extraneous and/or supererogatory textbooks.

In short, this PASSBOOK®, used directedly, should be an important factor in helping you to pass your test.

DATA ENTRY CLERK

DUTIES
Data Entry Clerks work under direct supervision and operate electronic data processing equipment to enter, retrieve, modify or transfer information. They also perform related office clerical duties

SUBJECT OF EXAMINATION
The written test will test for knowledge, skills, and/or abilities in such areas as:
1. Name and number checking; and
2. Filing.

HOW TO TAKE A TEST

I. YOU MUST PASS AN EXAMINATION

A. *WHAT EVERY CANDIDATE SHOULD KNOW*

Examination applicants often ask us for help in preparing for the written test. What can I study in advance? What kinds of questions will be asked? How will the test be given? How will the papers be graded?

As an applicant for a civil service examination, you may be wondering about some of these things. Our purpose here is to suggest effective methods of advance study and to describe civil service examinations.

Your chances for success on this examination can be increased if you know how to prepare. Those "pre-examination jitters" can be reduced if you know what to expect. You can even experience an adventure in good citizenship if you know why civil service exams are given.

B. *WHY ARE CIVIL SERVICE EXAMINATIONS GIVEN?*

Civil service examinations are important to you in two ways. As a citizen, you want public jobs filled by employees who know how to do their work. As a job seeker, you want a fair chance to compete for that job on an equal footing with other candidates. The best-known means of accomplishing this two-fold goal is the competitive examination.

Exams are widely publicized throughout the nation. They may be administered for jobs in federal, state, city, municipal, town or village governments or agencies.

Any citizen may apply, with some limitations, such as the age or residence of applicants. Your experience and education may be reviewed to see whether you meet the requirements for the particular examination. When these requirements exist, they are reasonable and applied consistently to all applicants. Thus, a competitive examination may cause you some uneasiness now, but it is your privilege and safeguard.

C. *HOW ARE CIVIL SERVICE EXAMS DEVELOPED?*

Examinations are carefully written by trained technicians who are specialists in the field known as "psychological measurement," in consultation with recognized authorities in the field of work that the test will cover. These experts recommend the subject matter areas or skills to be tested; only those knowledges or skills important to your success on the job are included. The most reliable books and source materials available are used as references. Together, the experts and technicians judge the difficulty level of the questions.

Test technicians know how to phrase questions so that the problem is clearly stated. Their ethics do not permit "trick" or "catch" questions. Questions may have been tried out on sample groups, or subjected to statistical analysis, to determine their usefulness.

Written tests are often used in combination with performance tests, ratings of training and experience, and oral interviews. All of these measures combine to form the best-known means of finding the right person for the right job.

II. HOW TO PASS THE WRITTEN TEST

A. NATURE OF THE EXAMINATION

To prepare intelligently for civil service examinations, you should know how they differ from school examinations you have taken. In school you were assigned certain definite pages to read or subjects to cover. The examination questions were quite detailed and usually emphasized memory. Civil service exams, on the other hand, try to discover your present ability to perform the duties of a position, plus your potentiality to learn these duties. In other words, a civil service exam attempts to predict how successful you will be. Questions cover such a broad area that they cannot be as minute and detailed as school exam questions.

In the public service similar kinds of work, or positions, are grouped together in one "class." This process is known as *position-classification*. All the positions in a class are paid according to the salary range for that class. One class title covers all of these positions, and they are all tested by the same examination.

B. FOUR BASIC STEPS

1) Study the announcement

How, then, can you know what subjects to study? Our best answer is: "Learn as much as possible about the class of positions for which you've applied." The exam will test the knowledge, skills and abilities needed to do the work.

Your most valuable source of information about the position you want is the official exam announcement. This announcement lists the training and experience qualifications. Check these standards and apply only if you come reasonably close to meeting them.

The brief description of the position in the examination announcement offers some clues to the subjects which will be tested. Think about the job itself. Review the duties in your mind. Can you perform them, or are there some in which you are rusty? Fill in the blank spots in your preparation.

Many jurisdictions preview the written test in the exam announcement by including a section called "Knowledge and Abilities Required," "Scope of the Examination," or some similar heading. Here you will find out specifically what fields will be tested.

2) Review your own background

Once you learn in general what the position is all about, and what you need to know to do the work, ask yourself which subjects you already know fairly well and which need improvement. You may wonder whether to concentrate on improving your strong areas or on building some background in your fields of weakness. When the announcement has specified "some knowledge" or "considerable knowledge," or has used adjectives like "beginning principles of…" or "advanced … methods," you can get a clue as to the number and difficulty of questions to be asked in any given field. More questions, and hence broader coverage, would be included for those subjects which are more important in the work. Now weigh your strengths and weaknesses against the job requirements and prepare accordingly.

3) Determine the level of the position

Another way to tell how intensively you should prepare is to understand the level of the job for which you are applying. Is it the entering level? In other words, is this the position in which beginners in a field of work are hired? Or is it an intermediate or advanced level? Sometimes this is indicated by such words as "Junior" or "Senior" in the class title. Other jurisdictions use Roman numerals to designate the level – Clerk I, Clerk II, for example. The word "Supervisor" sometimes appears in the title. If the level is not indicated by the title, check the description of duties. Will you be working under very close supervision, or will you have responsibility for independent decisions in this work?

4) Choose appropriate study materials

Now that you know the subjects to be examined and the relative amount of each subject to be covered, you can choose suitable study materials. For beginning level jobs, or even advanced ones, if you have a pronounced weakness in some aspect of your training, read a modern, standard textbook in that field. Be sure it is up to date and has general coverage. Such books are normally available at your library, and the librarian will be glad to help you locate one. For entry-level positions, questions of appropriate difficulty are chosen – neither highly advanced questions, nor those too simple. Such questions require careful thought but not advanced training.

If the position for which you are applying is technical or advanced, you will read more advanced, specialized material. If you are already familiar with the basic principles of your field, elementary textbooks would waste your time. Concentrate on advanced textbooks and technical periodicals. Think through the concepts and review difficult problems in your field.

These are all general sources. You can get more ideas on your own initiative, following these leads. For example, training manuals and publications of the government agency which employs workers in your field can be useful, particularly for technical and professional positions. A letter or visit to the government department involved may result in more specific study suggestions, and certainly will provide you with a more definite idea of the exact nature of the position you are seeking.

III. KINDS OF TESTS

Tests are used for purposes other than measuring knowledge and ability to perform specified duties. For some positions, it is equally important to test ability to make adjustments to new situations or to profit from training. In others, basic mental abilities not dependent on information are essential. Questions which test these things may not appear as pertinent to the duties of the position as those which test for knowledge and information. Yet they are often highly important parts of a fair examination. For very general questions, it is almost impossible to help you direct your study efforts. What we can do is to point out some of the more common of these general abilities needed in public service positions and describe some typical questions.

1) General information

Broad, general information has been found useful for predicting job success in some kinds of work. This is tested in a variety of ways, from vocabulary lists to questions about current events. Basic background in some field of work, such as sociology or economics, may be sampled in a group of questions. Often these are principles which have become familiar to most persons through exposure rather than through formal training. It is difficult to advise you how to study for these questions; being alert to the world around you is our best suggestion.

2) Verbal ability

An example of an ability needed in many positions is verbal or language ability. Verbal ability is, in brief, the ability to use and understand words. Vocabulary and grammar tests are typical measures of this ability. Reading comprehension or paragraph interpretation questions are common in many kinds of civil service tests. You are given a paragraph of written material and asked to find its central meaning.

3) Numerical ability
Number skills can be tested by the familiar arithmetic problem, by checking paired lists of numbers to see which are alike and which are different, or by interpreting charts and graphs. In the latter test, a graph may be printed in the test booklet which you are asked to use as the basis for answering questions.

4) Observation
A popular test for law-enforcement positions is the observation test. A picture is shown to you for several minutes, then taken away. Questions about the picture test your ability to observe both details and larger elements.

5) Following directions
In many positions in the public service, the employee must be able to carry out written instructions dependably and accurately. You may be given a chart with several columns, each column listing a variety of information. The questions require you to carry out directions involving the information given in the chart.

6) Skills and aptitudes
Performance tests effectively measure some manual skills and aptitudes. When the skill is one in which you are trained, such as typing or shorthand, you can practice. These tests are often very much like those given in business school or high school courses. For many of the other skills and aptitudes, however, no short-time preparation can be made. Skills and abilities natural to you or that you have developed throughout your lifetime are being tested.

Many of the general questions just described provide all the data needed to answer the questions and ask you to use your reasoning ability to find the answers. Your best preparation for these tests, as well as for tests of facts and ideas, is to be at your physical and mental best. You, no doubt, have your own methods of getting into an exam-taking mood and keeping "in shape." The next section lists some ideas on this subject.

IV. KINDS OF QUESTIONS

Only rarely is the "essay" question, which you answer in narrative form, used in civil service tests. Civil service tests are usually of the short-answer type. Full instructions for answering these questions will be given to you at the examination. But in case this is your first experience with short-answer questions and separate answer sheets, here is what you need to know:

1) Multiple-choice Questions
Most popular of the short-answer questions is the "multiple choice" or "best answer" question. It can be used, for example, to test for factual knowledge, ability to solve problems or judgment in meeting situations found at work.
A multiple-choice question is normally one of three types—
- It can begin with an incomplete statement followed by several possible endings. You are to find the one ending which *best* completes the statement, although some of the others may not be entirely wrong.
- It can also be a complete statement in the form of a question which is answered by choosing one of the statements listed.

- It can be in the form of a problem – again you select the best answer.

Here is an example of a multiple-choice question with a discussion which should give you some clues as to the method for choosing the right answer:

When an employee has a complaint about his assignment, the action which will *best* help him overcome his difficulty is to
- A. discuss his difficulty with his coworkers
- B. take the problem to the head of the organization
- C. take the problem to the person who gave him the assignment
- D. say nothing to anyone about his complaint

In answering this question, you should study each of the choices to find which is best. Consider choice "A" – Certainly an employee may discuss his complaint with fellow employees, but no change or improvement can result, and the complaint remains unresolved. Choice "B" is a poor choice since the head of the organization probably does not know what assignment you have been given, and taking your problem to him is known as "going over the head" of the supervisor. The supervisor, or person who made the assignment, is the person who can clarify it or correct any injustice. Choice "C" is, therefore, correct. To say nothing, as in choice "D," is unwise. Supervisors have and interest in knowing the problems employees are facing, and the employee is seeking a solution to his problem.

2) True/False Questions

The "true/false" or "right/wrong" form of question is sometimes used. Here a complete statement is given. Your job is to decide whether the statement is right or wrong.

SAMPLE: A roaming cell-phone call to a nearby city costs less than a non-roaming call to a distant city.

This statement is wrong, or false, since roaming calls are more expensive.

This is not a complete list of all possible question forms, although most of the others are variations of these common types. You will always get complete directions for answering questions. Be sure you understand *how* to mark your answers – ask questions until you do.

V. RECORDING YOUR ANSWERS

Computer terminals are used more and more today for many different kinds of exams.

For an examination with very few applicants, you may be told to record your answers in the test booklet itself. Separate answer sheets are much more common. If this separate answer sheet is to be scored by machine – and this is often the case – it is highly important that you mark your answers correctly in order to get credit.

An electronic scoring machine is often used in civil service offices because of the speed with which papers can be scored. Machine-scored answer sheets must be marked with a pencil, which will be given to you. This pencil has a high graphite content which responds to the electronic scoring machine. As a matter of fact, stray dots may register as answers, so do not let your pencil rest on the answer sheet while you are pondering the correct answer. Also, if your pencil lead breaks or is otherwise defective, ask for another.

Since the answer sheet will be dropped in a slot in the scoring machine, be careful not to bend the corners or get the paper crumpled.

The answer sheet normally has five vertical columns of numbers, with 30 numbers to a column. These numbers correspond to the question numbers in your test booklet. After each number, going across the page are four or five pairs of dotted lines. These short dotted lines have small letters or numbers above them. The first two pairs may also have a "T" or "F" above the letters. This indicates that the first two pairs only are to be used if the questions are of the true-false type. If the questions are multiple choice, disregard the "T" and "F" and pay attention only to the small letters or numbers.

Answer your questions in the manner of the sample that follows:

32. The largest city in the United States is
    A. Washington, D.C.
    B. New York City
    C. Chicago
    D. Detroit
    E. San Francisco

1) Choose the answer you think is best. (New York City is the largest, so "B" is correct.)
2) Find the row of dotted lines numbered the same as the question you are answering. (Find row number 32)
3) Find the pair of dotted lines corresponding to the answer. (Find the pair of lines under the mark "B.")
4) Make a solid black mark between the dotted lines.

VI. BEFORE THE TEST

Common sense will help you find procedures to follow to get ready for an examination. Too many of us, however, overlook these sensible measures. Indeed, nervousness and fatigue have been found to be the most serious reasons why applicants fail to do their best on civil service tests. Here is a list of reminders:

- Begin your preparation early – Don't wait until the last minute to go scurrying around for books and materials or to find out what the position is all about.
- Prepare continuously – An hour a night for a week is better than an all-night cram session. This has been definitely established. What is more, a night a week for a month will return better dividends than crowding your study into a shorter period of time.
- Locate the place of the exam – You have been sent a notice telling you when and where to report for the examination. If the location is in a different town or otherwise unfamiliar to you, it would be well to inquire the best route and learn something about the building.
- Relax the night before the test – Allow your mind to rest. Do not study at all that night. Plan some mild recreation or diversion; then go to bed early and get a good night's sleep.
- Get up early enough to make a leisurely trip to the place for the test – This way unforeseen events, traffic snarls, unfamiliar buildings, etc. will not upset you.
- Dress comfortably – A written test is not a fashion show. You will be known by number and not by name, so wear something comfortable.

- Leave excess paraphernalia at home – Shopping bags and odd bundles will get in your way. You need bring only the items mentioned in the official notice you received; usually everything you need is provided. Do not bring reference books to the exam. They will only confuse those last minutes and be taken away from you when in the test room.
- Arrive somewhat ahead of time – If because of transportation schedules you must get there very early, bring a newspaper or magazine to take your mind off yourself while waiting.
- Locate the examination room – When you have found the proper room, you will be directed to the seat or part of the room where you will sit. Sometimes you are given a sheet of instructions to read while you are waiting. Do not fill out any forms until you are told to do so; just read them and be prepared.
- Relax and prepare to listen to the instructions
- If you have any physical problem that may keep you from doing your best, be sure to tell the test administrator. If you are sick or in poor health, you really cannot do your best on the exam. You can come back and take the test some other time.

VII. AT THE TEST

The day of the test is here and you have the test booklet in your hand. The temptation to get going is very strong. Caution! There is more to success than knowing the right answers. You must know how to identify your papers and understand variations in the type of short-answer question used in this particular examination. Follow these suggestions for maximum results from your efforts:

1) Cooperate with the monitor

The test administrator has a duty to create a situation in which you can be as much at ease as possible. He will give instructions, tell you when to begin, check to see that you are marking your answer sheet correctly, and so on. He is not there to guard you, although he will see that your competitors do not take unfair advantage. He wants to help you do your best.

2) Listen to all instructions

Don't jump the gun! Wait until you understand all directions. In most civil service tests you get more time than you need to answer the questions. So don't be in a hurry. Read each word of instructions until you clearly understand the meaning. Study the examples, listen to all announcements and follow directions. Ask questions if you do not understand what to do.

3) Identify your papers

Civil service exams are usually identified by number only. You will be assigned a number; you must not put your name on your test papers. Be sure to copy your number correctly. Since more than one exam may be given, copy your exact examination title.

4) Plan your time

Unless you are told that a test is a "speed" or "rate of work" test, speed itself is usually not important. Time enough to answer all the questions will be provided, but this does not mean that you have all day. An overall time limit has been set. Divide the total time (in minutes) by the number of questions to determine the approximate time you have for each question.

5) Do not linger over difficult questions

If you come across a difficult question, mark it with a paper clip (useful to have along) and come back to it when you have been through the booklet. One caution if you do this – be sure to skip a number on your answer sheet as well. Check often to be sure that you have not lost your place and that you are marking in the row numbered the same as the question you are answering.

6) Read the questions

Be sure you know what the question asks! Many capable people are unsuccessful because they failed to *read* the questions correctly.

7) Answer all questions

Unless you have been instructed that a penalty will be deducted for incorrect answers, it is better to guess than to omit a question.

8) Speed tests

It is often better NOT to guess on speed tests. It has been found that on timed tests people are tempted to spend the last few seconds before time is called in marking answers at random – without even reading them – in the hope of picking up a few extra points. To discourage this practice, the instructions may warn you that your score will be "corrected" for guessing. That is, a penalty will be applied. The incorrect answers will be deducted from the correct ones, or some other penalty formula will be used.

9) Review your answers

If you finish before time is called, go back to the questions you guessed or omitted to give them further thought. Review other answers if you have time.

10) Return your test materials

If you are ready to leave before others have finished or time is called, take ALL your materials to the monitor and leave quietly. Never take any test material with you. The monitor can discover whose papers are not complete, and taking a test booklet may be grounds for disqualification.

VIII. EXAMINATION TECHNIQUES

1) Read the general instructions carefully. These are usually printed on the first page of the exam booklet. As a rule, these instructions refer to the timing of the examination; the fact that you should not start work until the signal and must stop work at a signal, etc. If there are any *special* instructions, such as a choice of questions to be answered, make sure that you note this instruction carefully.

2) When you are ready to start work on the examination, that is as soon as the signal has been given, read the instructions to each question booklet, underline any key words or phrases, such as *least, best, outline, describe* and the like. In this way you will tend to answer as requested rather than discover on reviewing your paper that you *listed without describing*, that you selected the *worst* choice rather than the *best* choice, etc.

3) If the examination is of the objective or multiple-choice type – that is, each question will also give a series of possible answers: A, B, C or D, and you are called upon to select the best answer and write the letter next to that answer on your answer paper – it is advisable to start answering each question in turn. There may be anywhere from 50 to 100 such questions in the three or four hours allotted and you can see how much time would be taken if you read through all the questions before beginning to answer any. Furthermore, if you come across a question or group of questions which you know would be difficult to answer, it would undoubtedly affect your handling of all the other questions.

4) If the examination is of the essay type and contains but a few questions, it is a moot point as to whether you should read all the questions before starting to answer any one. Of course, if you are given a choice – say five out of seven and the like – then it is essential to read all the questions so you can eliminate the two that are most difficult. If, however, you are asked to answer all the questions, there may be danger in trying to answer the easiest one first because you may find that you will spend too much time on it. The best technique is to answer the first question, then proceed to the second, etc.

5) Time your answers. Before the exam begins, write down the time it started, then add the time allowed for the examination and write down the time it must be completed, then divide the time available somewhat as follows:
    - If 3-1/2 hours are allowed, that would be 210 minutes. If you have 80 objective-type questions, that would be an average of 2-1/2 minutes per question. Allow yourself no more than 2 minutes per question, or a total of 160 minutes, which will permit about 50 minutes to review.
    - If for the time allotment of 210 minutes there are 7 essay questions to answer, that would average about 30 minutes a question. Give yourself only 25 minutes per question so that you have about 35 minutes to review.

6) The most important instruction is to *read each question* and make sure you know what is wanted. The second most important instruction is to *time yourself properly* so that you answer every question. The third most important instruction is to *answer every question*. Guess if you have to but include something for each question. Remember that you will receive no credit for a blank and will probably receive some credit if you write something in answer to an essay question. If you guess a letter – say "B" for a multiple-choice question – you may have guessed right. If you leave a blank as an answer to a multiple-choice question, the examiners may respect your feelings but it will not add a point to your score. Some exams may penalize you for wrong answers, so in such cases *only*, you may not want to guess unless you have some basis for your answer.

7) Suggestions
    a. Objective-type questions
        1. Examine the question booklet for proper sequence of pages and questions
        2. Read all instructions carefully
        3. Skip any question which seems too difficult; return to it after all other questions have been answered
        4. Apportion your time properly; do not spend too much time on any single question or group of questions

5. Note and underline key words – *all, most, fewest, least, best, worst, same, opposite,* etc.
6. Pay particular attention to negatives
7. Note unusual option, e.g., unduly long, short, complex, different or similar in content to the body of the question
8. Observe the use of "hedging" words – *probably, may, most likely,* etc.
9. Make sure that your answer is put next to the same number as the question
10. Do not second-guess unless you have good reason to believe the second answer is definitely more correct
11. Cross out original answer if you decide another answer is more accurate; do not erase until you are ready to hand your paper in
12. Answer all questions; guess unless instructed otherwise
13. Leave time for review

b. Essay questions
1. Read each question carefully
2. Determine exactly what is wanted. Underline key words or phrases.
3. Decide on outline or paragraph answer
4. Include many different points and elements unless asked to develop any one or two points or elements
5. Show impartiality by giving pros and cons unless directed to select one side only
6. Make and write down any assumptions you find necessary to answer the questions
7. Watch your English, grammar, punctuation and choice of words
8. Time your answers; don't crowd material

8) Answering the essay question

Most essay questions can be answered by framing the specific response around several key words or ideas. Here are a few such key words or ideas:

M's: manpower, materials, methods, money, management
P's: purpose, program, policy, plan, procedure, practice, problems, pitfalls, personnel, public relations

a. Six basic steps in handling problems:
1. Preliminary plan and background development
2. Collect information, data and facts
3. Analyze and interpret information, data and facts
4. Analyze and develop solutions as well as make recommendations
5. Prepare report and sell recommendations
6. Install recommendations and follow up effectiveness

b. Pitfalls to avoid
1. *Taking things for granted* – A statement of the situation does not necessarily imply that each of the elements is necessarily true; for example, a complaint may be invalid and biased so that all that can be taken for granted is that a complaint has been registered

2. *Considering only one side of a situation* – Wherever possible, indicate several alternatives and then point out the reasons you selected the best one
3. *Failing to indicate follow up* – Whenever your answer indicates action on your part, make certain that you will take proper follow-up action to see how successful your recommendations, procedures or actions turn out to be
4. *Taking too long in answering any single question* – Remember to time your answers properly

IX. AFTER THE TEST

Scoring procedures differ in detail among civil service jurisdictions although the general principles are the same. Whether the papers are hand-scored or graded by machine we have described, they are nearly always graded by number. That is, the person who marks the paper knows only the number – never the name – of the applicant. Not until all the papers have been graded will they be matched with names. If other tests, such as training and experience or oral interview ratings have been given, scores will be combined. Different parts of the examination usually have different weights. For example, the written test might count 60 percent of the final grade, and a rating of training and experience 40 percent. In many jurisdictions, veterans will have a certain number of points added to their grades.

After the final grade has been determined, the names are placed in grade order and an eligible list is established. There are various methods for resolving ties between those who get the same final grade – probably the most common is to place first the name of the person whose application was received first. Job offers are made from the eligible list in the order the names appear on it. You will be notified of your grade and your rank as soon as all these computations have been made. This will be done as rapidly as possible.

People who are found to meet the requirements in the announcement are called "eligibles." Their names are put on a list of eligible candidates. An eligible's chances of getting a job depend on how high he stands on this list and how fast agencies are filling jobs from the list.

When a job is to be filled from a list of eligibles, the agency asks for the names of people on the list of eligibles for that job. When the civil service commission receives this request, it sends to the agency the names of the three people highest on this list. Or, if the job to be filled has specialized requirements, the office sends the agency the names of the top three persons who meet these requirements from the general list.

The appointing officer makes a choice from among the three people whose names were sent to him. If the selected person accepts the appointment, the names of the others are put back on the list to be considered for future openings.

That is the rule in hiring from all kinds of eligible lists, whether they are for typist, carpenter, chemist, or something else. For every vacancy, the appointing officer has his choice of any one of the top three eligibles on the list. This explains why the person whose name is on top of the list sometimes does not get an appointment when some of the persons lower on the list do. If the appointing officer chooses the second or third eligible, the No. 1 eligible does not get a job at once, but stays on the list until he is appointed or the list is terminated.

X. HOW TO PASS THE INTERVIEW TEST

The examination for which you applied requires an oral interview test. You have already taken the written test and you are now being called for the interview test – the final part of the formal examination.

You may think that it is not possible to prepare for an interview test and that there are no procedures to follow during an interview. Our purpose is to point out some things you can do in advance that will help you and some good rules to follow and pitfalls to avoid while you are being interviewed.

What is an interview supposed to test?

The written examination is designed to test the technical knowledge and competence of the candidate; the oral is designed to evaluate intangible qualities, not readily measured otherwise, and to establish a list showing the relative fitness of each candidate – as measured against his competitors – for the position sought. Scoring is not on the basis of "right" and "wrong," but on a sliding scale of values ranging from "not passable" to "outstanding." As a matter of fact, it is possible to achieve a relatively low score without a single "incorrect" answer because of evident weakness in the qualities being measured.

Occasionally, an examination may consist entirely of an oral test – either an individual or a group oral. In such cases, information is sought concerning the technical knowledges and abilities of the candidate, since there has been no written examination for this purpose. More commonly, however, an oral test is used to supplement a written examination.

Who conducts interviews?

The composition of oral boards varies among different jurisdictions. In nearly all, a representative of the personnel department serves as chairman. One of the members of the board may be a representative of the department in which the candidate would work. In some cases, "outside experts" are used, and, frequently, a businessman or some other representative of the general public is asked to serve. Labor and management or other special groups may be represented. The aim is to secure the services of experts in the appropriate field.

However the board is composed, it is a good idea (and not at all improper or unethical) to ascertain in advance of the interview who the members are and what groups they represent. When you are introduced to them, you will have some idea of their backgrounds and interests, and at least you will not stutter and stammer over their names.

What should be done before the interview?

While knowledge about the board members is useful and takes some of the surprise element out of the interview, there is other preparation which is more substantive. It *is* possible to prepare for an oral interview – in several ways:

1) Keep a copy of your application and review it carefully before the interview

This may be the only document before the oral board, and the starting point of the interview. Know what education and experience you have listed there, and the sequence and dates of all of it. Sometimes the board will ask you to review the highlights of your experience for them; you should not have to hem and haw doing it.

2) Study the class specification and the examination announcement

Usually, the oral board has one or both of these to guide them. The qualities, characteristics or knowledges required by the position sought are stated in these documents. They offer valuable clues as to the nature of the oral interview. For example, if the job involves supervisory responsibilities, the announcement will usually indicate that knowledge of modern supervisory methods and the qualifications of the candidate as a supervisor will be tested. If so, you can expect such questions, frequently in the form of a hypothetical situation which you are expected to solve. NEVER go into an oral without knowledge of the duties and responsibilities of the job you seek.

3) Think through each qualification required

Try to visualize the kind of questions you would ask if you were a board member. How well could you answer them? Try especially to appraise your own knowledge and background in each area, *measured against the job sought*, and identify any areas in which you are weak. Be critical and realistic – do not flatter yourself.

4) Do some general reading in areas in which you feel you may be weak

For example, if the job involves supervision and your past experience has NOT, some general reading in supervisory methods and practices, particularly in the field of human relations, might be useful. Do NOT study agency procedures or detailed manuals. The oral board will be testing your understanding and capacity, not your memory.

5) Get a good night's sleep and watch your general health and mental attitude

You will want a clear head at the interview. Take care of a cold or any other minor ailment, and of course, no hangovers.

What should be done on the day of the interview?

Now comes the day of the interview itself. Give yourself plenty of time to get there. Plan to arrive somewhat ahead of the scheduled time, particularly if your appointment is in the fore part of the day. If a previous candidate fails to appear, the board might be ready for you a bit early. By early afternoon an oral board is almost invariably behind schedule if there are many candidates, and you may have to wait. Take along a book or magazine to read, or your application to review, but leave any extraneous material in the waiting room when you go in for your interview. In any event, relax and compose yourself.

The matter of dress is important. The board is forming impressions about you – from your experience, your manners, your attitude, and your appearance. Give your personal appearance careful attention. Dress your best, but not your flashiest. Choose conservative, appropriate clothing, and be sure it is immaculate. This is a business interview, and your appearance should indicate that you regard it as such. Besides, being well groomed and properly dressed will help boost your confidence.

Sooner or later, someone will call your name and escort you into the interview room. *This is it.* From here on you are on your own. It is too late for any more preparation. But remember, you asked for this opportunity to prove your fitness, and you are here because your request was granted.

What happens when you go in?

The usual sequence of events will be as follows: The clerk (who is often the board stenographer) will introduce you to the chairman of the oral board, who will introduce you to the other members of the board. Acknowledge the introductions before you sit down. Do not be surprised if you find a microphone facing you or a stenotypist sitting by. Oral interviews are usually recorded in the event of an appeal or other review.

Usually the chairman of the board will open the interview by reviewing the highlights of your education and work experience from your application – primarily for the benefit of the other members of the board, as well as to get the material into the record. Do not interrupt or comment unless there is an error or significant misinterpretation; if that is the case, do not hesitate. But do not quibble about insignificant matters. Also, he will usually ask you some question about your education, experience or your present job – partly to get you to start talking and to establish the interviewing "rapport." He may start the actual questioning, or turn it over to one of the other members. Frequently, each member undertakes the questioning on a particular area, one in which he is perhaps most competent, so you can expect each member to participate in the examination. Because time is limited, you may also expect some rather abrupt switches in the direction the questioning takes, so do not be upset by it. Normally, a board member will not pursue a single line of questioning unless he discovers a particular strength or weakness.

After each member has participated, the chairman will usually ask whether any member has any further questions, then will ask you if you have anything you wish to add. Unless you are expecting this question, it may floor you. Worse, it may start you off on an extended, extemporaneous speech. The board is not usually seeking more information. The question is principally to offer you a last opportunity to present further qualifications or to indicate that you have nothing to add. So, if you feel that a significant qualification or characteristic has been overlooked, it is proper to point it out in a sentence or so. Do not compliment the board on the thoroughness of their examination – they have been sketchy, and you know it. If you wish, merely say, "No thank you, I have nothing further to add." This is a point where you can "talk yourself out" of a good impression or fail to present an important bit of information. Remember, *you close the interview yourself.*

The chairman will then say, "That is all, Mr. _____, thank you." Do not be startled; the interview is over, and quicker than you think. Thank him, gather your belongings and take your leave. Save your sigh of relief for the other side of the door.

How to put your best foot forward

Throughout this entire process, you may feel that the board individually and collectively is trying to pierce your defenses, seek out your hidden weaknesses and embarrass and confuse you. Actually, this is not true. They are obliged to make an appraisal of your qualifications for the job you are seeking, and they want to see you in your best light. Remember, they must interview all candidates and a non-cooperative candidate may become a failure in spite of their best efforts to bring out his qualifications. Here are 15 suggestions that will help you:

1) Be natural – Keep your attitude confident, not cocky

If you are not confident that you can do the job, do not expect the board to be. Do not apologize for your weaknesses, try to bring out your strong points. The board is interested in a positive, not negative, presentation. Cockiness will antagonize any board member and make him wonder if you are covering up a weakness by a false show of strength.

2) Get comfortable, but don't lounge or sprawl

Sit erectly but not stiffly. A careless posture may lead the board to conclude that you are careless in other things, or at least that you are not impressed by the importance of the occasion. Either conclusion is natural, even if incorrect. Do not fuss with your clothing, a pencil or an ashtray. Your hands may occasionally be useful to emphasize a point; do not let them become a point of distraction.

3) Do not wisecrack or make small talk

This is a serious situation, and your attitude should show that you consider it as such. Further, the time of the board is limited – they do not want to waste it, and neither should you.

4) Do not exaggerate your experience or abilities

In the first place, from information in the application or other interviews and sources, the board may know more about you than you think. Secondly, you probably will not get away with it. An experienced board is rather adept at spotting such a situation, so do not take the chance.

5) If you know a board member, do not make a point of it, yet do not hide it

Certainly you are not fooling him, and probably not the other members of the board. Do not try to take advantage of your acquaintanceship – it will probably do you little good.

6) Do not dominate the interview

Let the board do that. They will give you the clues – do not assume that you have to do all the talking. Realize that the board has a number of questions to ask you, and do not try to take up all the interview time by showing off your extensive knowledge of the answer to the first one.

7) Be attentive

You only have 20 minutes or so, and you should keep your attention at its sharpest throughout. When a member is addressing a problem or question to you, give him your undivided attention. Address your reply principally to him, but do not exclude the other board members.

8) Do not interrupt

A board member may be stating a problem for you to analyze. He will ask you a question when the time comes. Let him state the problem, and wait for the question.

9) Make sure you understand the question

Do not try to answer until you are sure what the question is. If it is not clear, restate it in your own words or ask the board member to clarify it for you. However, do not haggle about minor elements.

10) Reply promptly but not hastily

A common entry on oral board rating sheets is "candidate responded readily," or "candidate hesitated in replies." Respond as promptly and quickly as you can, but do not jump to a hasty, ill-considered answer.

11) Do not be peremptory in your answers

A brief answer is proper – but do not fire your answer back. That is a losing game from your point of view. The board member can probably ask questions much faster than you can answer them.

12) Do not try to create the answer you think the board member wants

He is interested in what kind of mind you have and how it works – not in playing games. Furthermore, he can usually spot this practice and will actually grade you down on it.

13) Do not switch sides in your reply merely to agree with a board member

Frequently, a member will take a contrary position merely to draw you out and to see if you are willing and able to defend your point of view. Do not start a debate, yet do not surrender a good position. If a position is worth taking, it is worth defending.

14) Do not be afraid to admit an error in judgment if you are shown to be wrong

The board knows that you are forced to reply without any opportunity for careful consideration. Your answer may be demonstrably wrong. If so, admit it and get on with the interview.

15) Do not dwell at length on your present job

The opening question may relate to your present assignment. Answer the question but do not go into an extended discussion. You are being examined for a *new* job, not your present one. As a matter of fact, try to phrase ALL your answers in terms of the job for which you are being examined.

Basis of Rating

Probably you will forget most of these "do's" and "don'ts" when you walk into the oral interview room. Even remembering them all will not ensure you a passing grade. Perhaps you did not have the qualifications in the first place. But remembering them will help you to put your best foot forward, without treading on the toes of the board members.

Rumor and popular opinion to the contrary notwithstanding, an oral board wants you to make the best appearance possible. They know you are under pressure – but they also want to see how you respond to it as a guide to what your reaction would be under the pressures of the job you seek. They will be influenced by the degree of poise you display, the personal traits you show and the manner in which you respond.

ABOUT THIS BOOK

This book contains tests divided into Examination Sections. Go through each test, answering every question in the margin. We have also attached a sample answer sheet at the back of the book that can be removed and used. At the end of each test look at the answer key and check your answers. On the ones you got wrong, look at the right answer choice and learn. Do not fill in the answers first. Do not memorize the questions and answers, but understand the answer and principles involved. On your test, the questions will likely be different from the samples. Questions are changed and new ones added. If you understand these past questions you should have success with any changes that arise. Tests may consist of several types of questions. We have additional books on each subject should more study be advisable or necessary for you. Finally, the more you study, the better prepared you will be. This book is intended to be the last thing you study before you walk into the examination room. Prior study of relevant texts is also recommended. NLC publishes some of these in our Fundamental Series. Knowledge and good sense are important factors in passing your exam. Good luck also helps. So now study this Passbook, absorb the material contained within and take that knowledge into the examination. Then do your best to pass that exam.

EXAMINATION SECTION

CLERICAL ABILITIES TEST

Clerical aptitude involves the ability to perceive pertinent detail in verbal or tabular material, to observe differences in copy, to proofread words and numbers, and to avoid perceptual errors in arithmetic computation.

NATURE OF THE TEST

Four types of clerical aptitude questions are presented in the Clerical Abilities Test. There are 120 questions with a short time limit. The test contains 30 questions on name and number checking, 30 on the arrangement of names in correct alphabetical order, 30 on simple arithmetic, and 30 on inspecting groups of letters and numbers. The questions have been arranged in groups or cycles of five questions of each type. The Clerical Abilities Test is primarily a test of speed in carrying out relatively simple clerical tasks. While accuracy on these tasks is important and will be taken into account in the scoring, experience has shown that many persons are so concerned about accuracy that they do the test more slowly than they should. Competitors should be cautioned that speed as well as accuracy is important to achieve a good score.

HOW THE TEST IS ADMINISTERED

Each competitor should be given a copy of the test booklet with sample questions on the cover page, an answer sheet, and a medium No. 2 pencil. Ten minutes are allowed to study the directions and sample questions and to answer the questions in the proper boxes on the two pages.
The separate answer sheet should be used for the test proper. Fifteen minutes are allowed for the test.

HOW THE TEST IS SCORED

The correct answers should be counted and recorded. The number of incorrect answers must also be counted because one-fourth of the number of incorrect answers is subtracted from the number of right answers. An omission is considered as neither a right nor a wrong answer. The score on this test is the number of right answers minus one-fourth of the number of wrong answers (fractions of one-half or less are dropped). For example, if an applicant had answered 89 questions correctly and 10 questions incorrectly, and had omitted 1 question, his score would be 87.

EXAMINATION SECTION

DIRECTIONS: This test contains four kinds of questions. There are some of each kind on each page in the booklet. The time limit for the test will be announced by the examiner.
Use the special pencil furnished by the examiner in marking your answers on the separate answer sheet. For each question, there are five suggested answers. Decide which answer is correct, find the number of the question on the answer sheet, and make a solid black mark between the dotted lines just below the letter of your answer. If you wish to change your answer, erase the first mark completely, do not merely cross it out.

SAMPLE QUESTIONS

In each line across the page there are three names or numbers that are much alike. Compare the three names or numbers and decide which ones are exactly alike. On the Sample Answer Sheet at the right, mark the answer
- A. if ALL THREE names or numbers are exactly ALIKE
- B. if only the FIRST and SECOND names or numbers are exactly ALIKE
- C. if only the FIRST and THIRD names or numbers are exactly ALIKE
- D. if only the SECOND and THIRD names or numbers are exactly ALIKE
- E. if ALL THREE names or numbers are DIFFERENT

I.	Davis Hazen	David Hozen	David Hazen
II.	Lois Appel	Lois Appel	Lois Apfel
III.	June Allan	Jane Allan	Jane Allan
IV.	10235	10235	10235
V.	32614	32164	32614

It will be to your advantage to learn what A, B, C, D, and E stand for. If you finish the sample questions before you are told to turn to the test, study them.

In the next group of sample questions, there is a name in a box at the left, and four other names in alphabetical order at the right. Find the correct space for the boxed name so that it will be in alphabetical order with the others, and mark the letter of that space as your answer.

VI. | Jones, Jane |

A. →
Goodyear, G.L.
B. →
Haddon, Harry
C. →
Jackson, Mary
D. →
Jenkins, William
E. →

VII. | Kessler, Neilson |

A. →
Kessel, Carl
B. →
Kessinger, D.J.
C. →
Kessler, Karl
D. →
Kessner, Lewis
E. →

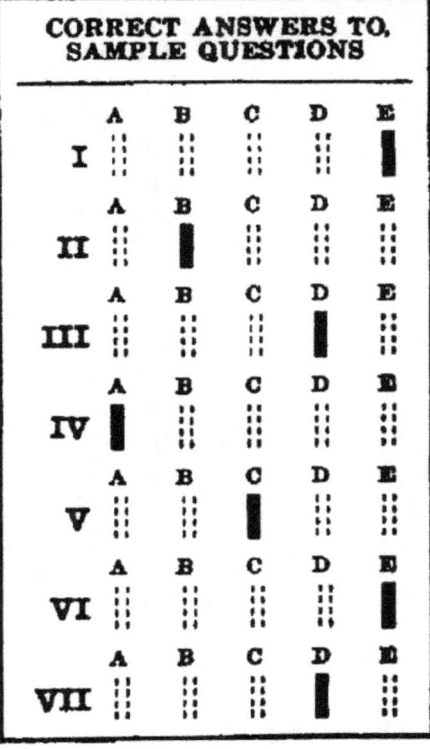

DIRECTIONS: In the following questions, complete the equation and find your answer among the list of suggested answers. Mark the Sample Answer Sheet A, B, C, or D for the answer you obtained; or if your answer is not among these, mark E for that question.

VIII. Add: 22
         +33

A. 44   B. 45   C. 54   D. 55   E. None of these

IX. Subtract: 24
            - 3

A. 20   B. 21   C. 27   D. 29   E. None of these

X. Multiply: 25
           x 5

A. 100   B. 115   C. 125   D. 135   E. None of these

XI. Divide: 6/126̄

    A. 20   B. 22   C. 24   D. 26   E. None of these

DIRECTIONS: There is one set of suggested answers for the next group of sample questions. Do not try to memorize these answers, because there will be a different set on each age in the test.

To find the answer to a question, find which suggested answer contains numbers and letters, all of which appear in the question. If no suggested answer fits, mark E for that question.

XII. 8 N K 9 G T 4 6

XIII. T 9 7 Z 6 L 3 K

XIV. Z 7 G K 3 9 8 N

XV. 3 K 9 4 6 G Z L

XVI. Z N 7 3 8 K T 9

Suggested Answers
A = 7, 9, G, K
B = 8, 9, T, Z
C = 6, 7, K, Z
D = 6, 8, G, T
E = None of the above

After you have marked your answers to all the questions on the Sample Answer Sheets on this page and on the front page of the booklet, check them with the answers in the boxes marked Correct Answers To Sample Questions.

Questions 1-5.

In Questions 1 through 5, compare the three names or numbers, and mark
    A. if ALL THREE names or numbers are exactly ALIKE
    B. if only the FIRST and SECOND names or numbers are exactly ALIKE
    C. if only the FIRST and THIRD names or numbers are exactly ALIKE
    D. if only the SECOND and THIRD names or numbers are exactly ALIKE
    E. if ALL THREE names or numbers are DIFFERENT

1. 5261383   5261383   5261338

2. 8125690   8126690   8125609

3. W.E. Johnston   W.E. Johnson   W.E. Johnson

4. Vergil L. Muller   Vergil L. Muller   Vergil L. Muller

5. Atherton R. Warde   Asheton R. Warde   Atherton P. Warde

Questions 6-10.

In Questions 6 through 10, find the correct place for the name in the box

6. Hackett, Gerald
   - A. →
     Habert, James
   - B. →
     Hachett, J.J.
   - C. →
     Hachetts, K. Larson
   - D. →
     Hachettson, Leroy
   - E. →

7. Margenroth, Alvin
   - A. →
     Margeroth, Albert
   - B. →
     Margestein, Dan
   - C. →
     Margestein, David
   - D. →
     Margue, Edgar
   - E. →

8. Bobbitt, Olivier E.
   - A. →
     Bobbitt, D. Olivier
   - B. →
     Bobbitt, Olivia B
   - C. →
     Bobbitt, Olivia H.
   - D. →
     Bobbitt, R. Olivia
   - E. →

9. Mosley, Werner
   - A. →
     Mosely, Albert J.
   - B. →
     Mosley, Alvin
   - C. →
     Mosley, S.M.
   - D. →
     Mozley, Vinson N.
   - E. →

10. | Youmuns, Frank L. |

A. →
Youmons, Frank G.
B. →
Youmons, Frank H.
C. →
Youmons, Frank K.
D. →
Youmons, Frank M.
E. →

Questions 11-15.

11. Add: 43
    +32

   A. 55   B. 65   C. 66   D. 75   E. None of these

12. Subtract: 83
    - 4

   A. 73   B. 79   C. 80   D. 89   E. None of these

13. Multiply: 41
    x 7

   A. 281   B. 287   C. 291   D. 297   E. None of these

14. Divide: 6/306

   A. 44   B. 51   C. 52   D. 60   E. None of these

15. Add: 37
    +15

   A. 42   B. 52   C. 53   D. 62   E. None of these

Questions 16-20.

In Questions 16 through 20, find which one of the suggested answers appears in that question.

16. 6 2 5 K 4 P T G

17. L 4 7 2 T 6 V K

18. 3 5 4 L 9 V T G

19. G 4 K 7 L 3 5 Z

SUGGESTED ANSWERS
A = 4, 5, K, T
B = 4, 7, G, K
C = 2, 5, G, L
D = 2, 7, L, T
E = None of the above

20. 4 K 2 9 N 5 T G

Questions 21-25.

In Questions 21 through 25, compare the three names or numbers, and mark
   A. if ALL THREE names or numbers are exactly ALIKE
   B. if only the FIRST and SECOND names or numbers are exactly ALIKE
   C. if only the FIRST and THIRD names or numbers are exactly ALIKE
   D. if only the SECOND and THIRD names or numbers are exactly ALIKE
   E. if ALL THREE names or numbers are DIFFERENT

21.	2395890	2395890	2395890
22.	1926341	1926347	1926314
23.	E. Owens McVey	E. Owen McVey	E. Owen McVay
24.	Emily Neal Rouse	Emily Neal Rowse	Emily Neal Rowse
25.	H. Merritt Audubon	H. Merriott Audubon	H. Merritt Audubon

Questions 26-30.

In Questions 26 through 30, find the correct place for the name in the box.

26. Watters, N.O.

   A. →
       Waters, Charles L.
   B. →
       Waterson, Nina P.
   C. →
       Watson, Nora J.
   D. →
       Wattwood, Paul A.
   E. →

27. Johnston, Edward

   A. →
       Johnston, Edgar R.
   B. →
       Johnston, Edmond
   C. →
       Johnston, Edmund
   D. →
       Johnstone, Edmund A.
   E. →

28. Rensch, Adeline

A. →
Ramsay, Amos
B. →
Remschel, Augusta
C. →
Renshaw, Austin
D. →
Rentzel, Becky
E. →

29. Schnyder, Maurice

A. →
Schneider, Martin
B. →
Schneider, Mertens
C. →
Schnyder, Newman
D. →
Schreibner, Norman
E. →

30. Freedenburg, C. Erma

A. →
Freedenberg, Emerson
B. →
Freedenberg, Erma
C. →
Freedenberg, Erma E.
D. →
Freedinberg, Erma F.
E. →

Questions 31-35.

31. Subtract: 68
              - 47

    A. 10   B. 11   C. 20   D. 22   E. None of these

32. Multiply: 50
              x 8

    A. 400   B. 408   C. 450   D. 458   E. None of these

33. Divide: 9/180

    A. 20   B. 29   C. 30   D. 39   E. None of these

34. Add: 78
             + 63

    A. 131   B. 140   C. 141   D. 151   E. None of these

35. Add: 89
         - 70

   A. 9   B. 18   C. 19   D. 29   E. None of these

Questions 36-40.

In Questions 36 through 40, find which one of the suggested answers appears in that question.

36. 9 G Z 3 L 4 6 N

37. L 5 N K 4 3 9 V

38. 8 2 V P 9 L Z 5

39. V P 9 Z 5 L 8 7

40. 5 T 8 N 2 9 V L

SUGGESTED ANSWERS
A = 4, 9, L, V
B = 4, 5, N, Z
C = 5, 8, L, Z
D = 8, 9, N, V
E = None of the above

Questions 41-45.

In Questions 41 through 45, compare the three names or numbers, and mark
   A. if ALL THREE names or numbers are exactly ALIKE
   B. if only the FIRST and SECOND names or numbers are exactly ALIKE
   C. if only the FIRST and THIRD names or numbers are exactly ALIKE
   D. if only the SECOND and THIRD names or numbers are exactly ALIKE
   E. if ALL THREE names or numbers are DIFFERENT

41.	6219354	621354	6219354
42.	2312793	2312793	2312793
43.	1065407	1065407	1065047
44.	Francis Ransdell	Frances Ramsdell	Francis Ramsdell
45.	Cornelius Detwiler	Cornelius Detwiler	Cornelius Detwiler

Questions 46-50.

In Questions 46 through 50, find the correct place for the name in the box.

46. DeMattia, Jessica

A. →
DeLong, Jesse
B. →
DeMatteo, Jessie
C. →
Derby, Jessie S.
D. →
DeShazo, L.M.
E. →

47. Theriault, Louis

A. →
Therien, Annette
B. →
Therien, Elaine
C. →
Thibeault, Gerald
D. →
Thiebeault, Pierre
E. →

48. Gaston, M. Hubert

A. →
Gaston, Dorothy M.
B. →
Gaston, Henry N.
C. →
Gaston, Isabel
D. →
Gaston, M. Melvin
E. →

49. SanMiguel, Carlos

A. →
SanLuis, Juana
B. →
Santilli, Laura
C. →
Stinnett, Nellie
D. →
Stoddard, Victor
E. →

50. | DeLaTour, Hall F. | A. →
   DeLargy, Harold
   B. →
   DeLathouder, Hilda
   C. →
   Lathrop, Hillary
   D. →
   LaTour, Hulbert E.
   E. →

Questions 51-55.

51. Multiply: 62
    x 5

    A. 300   B. 310   C. 315   D. 360   E. None of these

52. Divide: 3/153

    A. 41   B. 43   C. 51   D. 53   E. None of these

53. Add: 47
    +21

    A. 58   B. 59   C. 67   D. 68   E. None of these

54. Subtract: 87
    - 42

    A. 34   B. 35   C. 44   D. 45   E. None of these

55. Multiply: 37
    x 3

    A. 91   B. 101   C. 104   D. 114   E. None of these

Questions 56-60.

For Questions 56 through 60, find which one of the suggested answers appears in that question.

56. N 5 4 7 T K 3 Z

57. 8 5 3 V L 2 Z N

58. 7 2 5 N 9 K L V

59. 9 8 L 2 5 Z K V

60. Z 6 5 V 9 3 P N

SUGGESTED ANSWERS
A = 3, 8, K, N
B = 5, 8, N, V
C = 3, 9, V, Z
D = 5, 9, K, Z
E = None of the above

Questions 61-65.

In Questions 61 through 65, compare the three names or numbers, and mark
    A. if ALL THREE names or numbers are exactly ALIKE
    B. if only the FIRST and SECOND names or numbers are exactly ALIKE
    C. if only the FIRST and THIRD names or numbers are exactly ALIKE
    D. if only the SECOND and THIRD names or numbers are exactly ALIKE
    E. if ALL THREE names or numbers are DIFFERENT

61. 6452054   6452654   6452054

62. 8501268   8501268   8501286

63. Ella Burk Newham   Ella Burk Newnham   Elena Burk Newnham

64. Jno. K. Ravencroft   Jno. H. Ravencroft   Jno. H. Ravencoft

65. Martin Wills Pullen   Martin Wills Pulen   Martin Wills Pullen

Questions 66-70.

In Questions 66 through 70, find the correct place for the name in the box.

66. | O'Bannon, M.J. |

    A. →
       O'Beirne, B.B.
    B. →
       Oberlin, E.L.
    C. →
       Oberneir, L.P.
    D. →
       O'Brian, S.F.
    E. →

67. | Entsminger, Jacob |

    A. →
       Ensminger, J.
    B. →
       Entsminger, J.A.
    C. →
       Entsminger, Jack
    D. →
       Entsminger, James
    E. →

68. | Iacone, Pete R. |
- A. →
  Iacone, Pedro
- B. →
  Iacone, Pedro M.
- C. →
  Iacone, Peter F.
- D. →
  Iascone, Peter W.
- E. →

69. | Sheppard, Gladys |
- A. →
  Shepard, Dwight
- B. →
  Shepard, F.H.
- C. →
  Shephard, Louise
- D. →
  Shepperd, Stella
- E. →

70. | Thackton, Melvin T. |
- A. →
  Thackston, Milton G.
- B. →
  Thackston, Milton W.
- C. →
  Thackston, Theodore
- D. →
  Thackston, Thomas G.
- E. →

Questions 71-75.

71. Divide: $7\overline{)357}$

    A. 51   B. 52   C. 53   D. 54   E. None of these

72. Add: 58
         +27

    A. 75   B. 84   C. 85   D. 95   E. None of these

73. Subtract: 86
              - 57

    A. 18   B. 29   C. 38   D. 39   E. None of these

74. Multiply: 68
              x 4

   A. 242   B. 264   C. 272   D. 274   E. None of these

75. Divide: 9/639̄

   A. 71   B. 73   C. 81   D. 83   E. None of these

Questions 76-80.

For Questions 76 through 80, find which one of the suggested answers appears in that question.

76. 6 Z T N 8 7 4 V

77. V 7 8 6 N 5 P L

78. N 7 P V 8 4 2 L

79. 7 8 G 4 3 V L T

80. 4 8 G 2 T N 6 L

SUGGESTED ANSWERS
A = 2, 7, L, N
B = 2, 8, T, V
C = 6, 8, L, T
D = 6, 7, N, V
E = None of the above

Questions 81-85.

In Questions 81 through 85, compare the three names or numbers, and mark
   A. if ALL THREE names or numbers are exactly ALIKE
   B. if only the FIRST and SECOND names or numbers are exactly ALIKE
   C. if only the FIRST and THIRD names or numbers are exactly ALIKE
   D. if only the SECOND and THIRD names or numbers are exactly ALIKE
   E. if ALL THREE names or numbers are DIFFERENT

81. 3457988	3457986	3457986
82. 4695682	4695862	4695682
83. Stricklund Kanedy	Stricklund Kanedy	Stricklund Kanedy
84. Joy Harbor Witner	Joy Harloe Witner	Joy Harloe Witner
85. R.M.O. Uberroth	R.M.O. Uberroth	R.N.O. Uberroth

Questions 86-90.

In Questions 86 through 90, find the correct place for the name in the box.

86. Dunlavey, M. Hilary

A. →
Dunleavy, Hilary G.
B. →
Dunleavy, Hilary K.
C. →
Dunleavy, Hilary S.
D. →
Dunleavy, Hilery W.
E. →

87. Yarbrough, Maria

A. →
Yabroudy, Margy
B. →
Yarboro, Marie
C. →
Yarborough, Marina
D. →
Yarborough, Mary
E. →

88. Prouty, Martha

A. →
Proutey, Margaret
B. →
Proutey, Maude
C. →
Prouty, Myra
D. →
Prouty, Naomi
E. →

89. Pawlowicz, Ruth M.

A. →
Pawalek, Edward
B. →
Pawelek, Flora G.
C. →
Pawlowski, Joan M.
D. →
Pawtowski, Wanda
E. →

90. | Vanstory, George |

A. →
   Vanover, Eva
B. →
   VanSwinderen, Floyd
C. →
   VanSyckle, Harry
D. →
   Vanture, Laurence
E. →

Questions 91-95

91. Add: 28
         +35

   A. 53   B. 62   C. 64   D. 73   E. None of these

92. Subtract: 78
              -69

   A. 7   B. 8   C. 18   D. 19   E. None of these

93. Multiply: 86
              x 6

   A. 492   B. 506   C. 516   D. 526   E. None of these

94. Divide: 8/648

   A. 71   B. 76   C. 81   D. 89   E. None of these

95. Add: 97
         +34

   A. 131   B. 132   C. 140   D. 141   E. None of these

Questions 96-100.

For Questions 96 through 100, find which one of the suggested answers appears in that question.

96. V 5 7 Z N 9 4 T

97. 4 6 P T 2 N K 9

98. 6 4 N 2 P 8 Z K

99. 7 P 5 2 4 N K T

100. K T 8 5 4 N 2 P

SUGGESTED ANSWERS
A = 2, 5, N, Z
B = 4, 5, N, P
C = 2, 9, P, T
D = 4, 9, T, Z
E = None of the above

Questions 101-105.

In Questions 101 through 105, compare the three names or numbers, and mark
- A. if ALL THREE names or numbers are exactly ALIKE
- B. if only the FIRST and SECOND names or numbers are exactly ALIKE
- C. if only the FIRST and THIRD names or numbers are exactly ALIKE
- D. if only the SECOND and THIRD names or numbers are exactly ALIKE
- E. if ALL THREE names or numbers are DIFFERENT

101. 1592514   1592574   1592574

102. 2010202   2010202   2010220

103. 6177396   6177936   6177396

104. Drusilla S. Ridgeley   Drusilla S. Ridgeley   Drusilla S. Ridgeley

105. Andrei I. Toumantzev   Andrei I. Tourmantzev   Andrei I. Toumantzov

Questions 106-110.

In Questions 106 through 110, find the correct place for the name in the box.

106. Fitzsimmons, Hugh
- A. →
  Fitts, Harold
- B. →
  Fitzgerald, June
- C. →
  FitzGibbon, Junius
- D. →
  FitzSimons, Martin
- E. →

107. D'Amato, Vincent
- A. →
  Daly, Steven
- B. →
  D'Amboise, S. Vincent
- C. →
  Daniel, Vail
- D. →
  DeAlba, Valentina
- E. →

108. Schaeffer, Roger D.

   A. →
   Schaffert, Evelyn M.
   B. →
   Schaffner, Margaret M.
   C. →
   Schafhirt, Milton G.
   D. →
   Shafer, Richard E.
   E. →

109. White-Lewis, Cecil

   A. →
   Whitelaw, Cordelia
   B. →
   White-Leigh, Nancy
   C. →
   Whitely, Rodney
   D. →
   Whitlock, Warren
   E. →

110. VanDerHeggen, Don

   A. →
   VanDemark, Doris
   B. →
   Vandenberg, H.E.
   C. →
   VanDercook, Marie
   D. →
   vanderLinden, Robert
   E. →

Questions 111-115.

111. Add: 75
            +49

   A. 124   B. 125   C. 134   D. 225   E. None of these

112. Subtract: 69
                 - 45

   A. 14   B. 23   C. 24   D. 26   E. None of these

113. Multiply: 36
                 x 8

   A. 246   B. 262   C. 288   D. 368   E. None of these

114. Divide: 8/328̄

    A. 31   B. 41   C. 42   D. 48   E. None of these

115. Multiply: 58
              x 9

    A. 472   B. 513   C. 521   D. 522   E. None of these

Questions 116-120.

For Questions 116 through 120, find which one of the suggested answers appears in that question.

116. Z 3 N P G 5 4 2

117. 6 N 2 8 G 4 P T

118. 6 N 4 T V G 8 2

119. T 3 P 4 N 8 G 2

120. 6 7 K G N 2 L 5

SUGGESTED ANSWERS:
A = 2, 3, G, N
B = 2, 6, N, T
C = 3, 4, G, K
D = 4, 6, K, T
E = None of the above

KEY (CORRECT ANSWERS)

1. B	21. A	41. A	61. C	81. D	101. D
2. E	22. E	42. A	62. B	82. C	102. B
3. D	23. E	43. B	63. E	83. A	103. C
4. A	24. D	44. E	64. E	84. D	104. A
5. E	25. C	45. A	65. C	85. B	105. E
6. E	26. D	46. C	66. A	86. A	106. D
7. A	27. D	47. A	667. D	87. E	107. B
8. D	28. C	48. D	68. C	88. C	108. A
9. B	29. C	49. B	69. D	89. C	109. C
10. E	30. D	50. C	70. E	90. B	110. D
11. D	31. E	51. B	71. A	91. E	111. A
12. B	32. A	52. C	72. C	92. E	112. C
13. B	33. A	53. D	73. B	93. C	113. C
14. B	34. C	54. D	74. C	94. C	114. B
15. B	35. C	55. E	75. A	95. A	115. D
16. A	36. E	56. E	76. D	96. D	116. A
17. D	37. A	57. B	77. D	97. C	117. B
18. E	38. C	58. E	78. A	98. E	118. B
19. B	39. C	59. D	79. E	99. B	119. A
20. A	40. D	60. C	80. C	100. B	120. E

CLERICAL ABILITIES
EXAMINATION SECTION
TEST 1

DIRECTIONS: Each question or incomplete statement is followed by several suggested answers or completions. Select the one that BEST answers the question or completes the statement. *PRINT THE LETTER OF THE CORRECT ANSWER IN THE SPACE AT THE RIGHT.*

Questions 1-4.

DIRECTIONS: Questions 1 through 4 are to be answered on the basis of the information given below.

The most commonly used filing system and the one that is easiest to learn is alphabetical filing. This involves putting records in an A to Z order, according to the letters of the alphabet. The name of a person is filed by using the following order: first, the surname or last name; second, the first name; third, the middle name or middle initial. For example, *Henry C. Young* is filed under *Y* and thereafter under *Young, Henry C.* The name of a company is filed in the same way. For example, *Long Cabinet Co.* is filed under *L* while *John T. Long Cabinet Co.* is filed under *L* and thereafter under *Long, John T. Cabinet Co.*

1. The one of the following which lists the names of persons in the CORRECT alphabetical order is:
    A. Mary Carrie, Helen Carrol, James Carson, John Carter
    B. James Carson, Mary Carrie, John Carter, Helen Carrol
    C. Helen Carrol, James Carson, John Carter, Mary Carrie
    D. John Carter, Helen Carrol, Mary Carrie, James Carson

1.____

2. The one of the following which lists the names of persons in the CORRECT alphabetical order is:
    A. Jones, John C.; Jones, John A.; Jones, John P.; Jones, John K.
    B. Jones, John P.; Jones, John K.; Jones, John C.; Jones, John A.
    C. Jones, John A.; Jones, John C.; Jones, John K.; Jones, John P.
    D. Jones, John K.; Jones, John C.; Jones, John A.; Jones, John P.

2.____

3. The one of the following which lists the names of the companies in the CORRECT alphabetical order is:
    A. Blane Co., Blake Co., Block Co., Blear Co.
    B. Blake Co., Blane Co., Blear Co., Block Co.
    C. Block Co., Blear Co., Blane Co., Blake Co.
    D. Blear Co., Blake Co., Blane Co., Block Co.

3.____

4. You are to return to the file an index card on *Barry C. Wayne Materials and Supplies Co.*
Of the following, the CORRECT alphabetical group that you should return the index card to is
A. A to G   B. H to M   C. N to S   D. T to Z

4.____

Questions 5-10.

DIRECTIONS: In each of Questions 5 through 10, the names of four people are given. For each question, choose as your answer the one of the four names given which should be filed FIRST according to the usual system of alphabetical filing of names, as described in the following paragraph.

In filing names, you must start with the last name. Names are filed in order of the first letter of the last name, then the second letter, etc. Therefore, BAILY would be filed before BROWN, which would be filed before COLT. A name with fewer letters of the same type comes first, i.e., Smith before Smithe. If the last names are the same, the names are filed alphabetically by the first name. If the first name is an initial, a name with an initial would come before a first name that starts with the same letter as the initial. Therefore, I. BROWN would come before IRA BROWN. Finally, if both last name and first name are the same, the name would be filed alphabetically by the middle name, once again an initial coming before a middle name which starts with the same letter as the initial. If there is no middle name at all, the name would come before those with middle initials or names.

SAMPLE QUESTION:
A. Lester Daniels
B. William Dancer
C. Nathan Danzig
D. Dan Lester

The last names beginning with D are filed before the last name beginning with L. Since DANIELS, DANCER, and DANZIG all begin with the same three letters, you must look at the fourth letter of the last name to determine which name should be filed first. C comes before I or Z in the alphabet, so DANCER is filed before DANIELS or DANZIG. Therefore, the answer to the above sample question is B.

5. A. Scott Biala
    B. Mary Byala
    C. Martin Baylor
    D. Francis Bauer

5.____

6. A. Howard J. Black
    B. Howard Black
    C. J. Howard Black
    D. John H. Black

6.____

7. A. Theodora Garth Kingston
    B. Theadore Barth Kingston
    C. Thomas Kingston
    D. Thomas T. Kingston

7.____

8. A. Paulette Mary Huerta
    B. Paul M. Huerta
    C. Paulette L. Huerta
    D. Peter A. Huerta

9. A. Martha Hunt Morgan
    B. Martin Hunt Morgan
    C. Mary H. Morgan
    D. Martine H. Morgan

10. A. James T. Meerschaum
    B. James M. Mershum
    C. James F. Mearshaum
    D. James N. Meshum

Questions 11-14.

DIRECTIONS: Questions 11 through 14 are to be answered SOLELY on the basis of the following information.

You are required to file various documents in file drawers which are labeled according to the following pattern:

DOCUMENTS

MEMOS		LETTERS	
File	Subject	File	Subject
84PM1	(A-L)	84PC1	(A-L)
84PM2	(M-Z)	84PC2	(M-Z)

REPORTS		INQUIRIES	
File	Subject	File	Subject
84PR1	(A-L)	84PQ1	(A-L)
84PR2	(M-Z)	84PQ2	(M-Z)

11. A letter dealing with a burglary should be filed in the drawer labeled
    A. 84PM1   B. 84PC1   C. 84PR1   D. 84PQ2

12. A report on Statistics should be found in the drawer labeled
    A. 84PM1   B. 84PC2   C. 84PR2   D. 84PQS

13. An inquiry is received about parade permit procedures. It should be filed in the drawer labeled
    A. 84PM2   B. 84PC1   C. 84PR1   D. 84PQ2

14. A police officer has a question about a robbery report you filed. You should pull this file from the drawer labeled
    A. 84PM1   B. 84PM2   C. 84PR1   D. 84PR2

Questions 15-22.

DIRECTIONS: Each of Questions 15 through 22 consists of four or six numbered names. For each question, choose the option (A, B, C, or D) which indicates the order in which the names should be filed in accordance with the following filing instructions:
- File alphabetically according to last name, then first name, then middle initial.
- File according to each successive letter within a name.
- When comparing two names in which the letters in the longer name are identical to the corresponding letters in the shorter name, the shorter name is filed first.
- When the last names are the same, initials are always filed before names beginning with the same letter.

15. I. Ralph Robinson
    II. Alfred Ross
    III. Luis Robles
    IV. James Roberts

    The CORRECT filing sequence for the above names should be
    A. IV, II, I, III   B. I, IV, III, II   C. III, IV, I, II   D. IV, I, III, II

16. I. Irwin Goodwin
    II. Inez Gonzalez
    III. Irene Goodman
    IV. Ira S. Goodwin
    V. Ruth I. Goldstein
    VI. M.B. Goodman

    The CORRECT filing sequence for the above names should be
    A. V, II, I, IV, III, VI
    B. V, II, VI, III, IV, I
    C. V, II, III, VI, IV, I
    D. V, II, III, VI, I, IV

17. I. George Allan
    II. Gregory Allen
    III. Gary Allen
    IV. George Allen

    The CORRECT filing sequence for the above names should be
    A. IV, III, I, II   B. I, IV, II, III   C. III, IV, I, II   D. I, III, IV, II

5 (#1)

18.
   I. Simon Kauffman
   II. Leo Kaufman
   III. Robert Kaufmann
   IV. Paul Kauffmann

   The CORRECT filing sequence for the above names should be
   A. I, IV, II, III   B. II, IV, III, I   C. III, II, IV, I   D. I, II, III, IV

   18.____

19.
   I. Roberta Williams
   II. Robin Wilson
   III. Roberta Wilson
   IV. Robin Williams

   The CORRECT filing sequence for the above names should be
   A. III, II, IV, I   B. I, IV, III, II   C. I, II, III, IV   D. III, I, II, IV

   19.____

20.
   I. Lawrence Shultz
   II. Albert Schultz
   III. Theodore Schwartz
   IV. Thomas Schwarz
   V. Alvin Schultz
   VI. Leonard Shultz

   The CORRECT filing sequence for the above names should be
   A. II, V, III, IV, I, VI   B. IV, III, V, I, II, VI
   C. II, V, I, VI, III, IV   D. I, VI, II, V, III, IV

   20.____

21.
   I. McArdle
   II. Mayer
   III. Maletz
   IV. McNiff
   V. Meyer
   VI. MacMahon

   The CORRECT filing sequence for the above names should be
   A. I, IV, VI, III, II, V   B. II, I, IV, VI, III, V
   C. VI, III, II, I, IV, V   D. VI, III, II, V, I, IV

   21.____

22.
   I. Jack E. Johnson
   II. R.H. Jackson
   III. Bertha Jackson
   IV. J.T. Johnson
   V. Ann Johns
   VI. John Jacobs

   The CORRECT filing sequence for the above names should be
   A. II, III, VI, V, IV, I   B. III, II, VI, V, IV, I
   C. VI, II, III, I, V, IV   D. III, II, VI, IV, V, I

   22.____

Questions 23-30.

DIRECTIONS: The code table below shows 10 letters with matching numbers. For each question, there are three sets of letters. Each set of letters is followed by a set of numbers which may or may not match their correct letter according to the code table. For each question, check all three sets of letters and numbers and mark your answer:
- A. if no pairs are correctly matched
- B. if only one pair is correctly matched
- C. if only two pairs are correctly matched
- D. if all three pairs are correctly matched

CODE TABLE

T	M	V	D	S	P	R	G	B	H
1	2	3	4	5	6	7	8	9	0

SAMPLE QUESTION: TMVDSP – 123456
RGBHTM – 789011
DSPRGB – 256789

In the sample question above, the first set of numbers correctly match its set of letters. But the second and third pairs contain mistakes. In the second pair, M is correctly matched with number 1. According to the code table, letter M should be correctly matched with number 2. In the third pair, the letter D is incorrectly matched with number 2. According to the code table, letter D should be correctly matched with number 4. Since only one of the pairs is correctly matched, the answer to this sample question is B.

23. RSBMRM – 759262
    GDSRVH – 845730
    VDBRTM - 349713

24. TGVSDR – 183247
    SMHRDP – 520647
    TRMHSR - 172057

25. DSPRGM – 456782
    MVDBHT – 234902
    HPMDBT - 062491

26. BVPTRD – 936184
    GDPHMB – 807029
    GMRHMV - 827032

27. MGVRSH – 283750
    TRDMBS – 174295
    SPRMGV - 567283

28. SGBSDM – 489542　　　　　　　　　　　　　　　　　　　　　　　28._____
    MGHPTM – 290612
    MPBMHT - 269301

29. TDPBHM – 146902　　　　　　　　　　　　　　　　　　　　　　　29._____
    VPBMRS – 369275
    GDMBHM - 842902

30. MVPTBV – 236194　　　　　　　　　　　　　　　　　　　　　　　30._____
    PDRTMB – 47128
    BGTMSM - 981232

KEY (CORRECT ANSWERS)

1.	A	11.	B	21.	C
2.	C	12.	C	22.	B
3.	B	13.	D	23.	B
4.	D	14.	D	24.	B
5.	D	15.	D	25.	C
6.	B	16.	C	26.	A
7.	B	17.	D	27.	D
8.	B	18.	A	28.	A
9.	A	19.	B	29.	D
10.	C	20.	A	30.	A

TEST 2

DIRECTIONS: Each question or incomplete statement is followed by several suggested answers or completions. Select the one that BEST answers the question or completes the statement. *PRINT THE LETTER OF THE CORRECT ANSWER IN THE SPACE AT THE RIGHT.*

Questions 1-10.

DIRECTIONS: Questions 1 through 10 each consists of two columns, each containing four lines of names, numbers and/or addresses. For each question, compare the lines in Column I with the lines in Column II to see if they match exactly, and mark your answer A, B, C, or D, according to the following instructions:
    A. all four lines match exactly
    B. only three lines match exactly
    C. only two lines match exactly
    D. only one line matches exactly

	COLUMN I	COLUMN II	
1.	I. Earl Hodgson II. 1409870 III. Shore Ave. IV. Macon Rd.	Earl Hodgson 1408970 Schore Ave. Macon Rd.	1.____
2.	I. 9671485 II. 470 Astor Court III. Halprin, Phillip IV. Frank D. Poliseo	9671485 470 Astor Court Halperin, Phillip Frank D. Poliseo	2.____
3.	I. Tandem Associates II. 144-17 Northern Blvd. III. Alberta Forchi IV. Kings Park, NY 10751	Tandom Associates 144-17 Northern Blvd. Albert Forchi Kings Point, NY 10751	3.____
4.	I. Bertha C. McCormack II. Clayton, MO III. 976-4242 IV. New City, NY 10951	Bertha C. McCormack Clayton, MO 976-4242 New City, NY 10951	4.____
5.	I. George C. Morill II. Columbia, SC 29201 III. Louis Ingham IV. 3406 Forest Ave.	George C. Morrill Columbia, SD 29201 Louis Ingham 3406 Forest Ave.	5.____
6.	I. 506 S. Elliott Pl. II. Herbert Hall III. 4712 Rockaway Pkway IV. 169 E. 7 St.	506 S. Elliott Pl. Hurbert Hall 4712 Rockaway Pkway 169 E. 7 St.	6.____

7. I.   345 Park Ave.   345 Park Pl.   7._____
    II. Colman Oven Corp.   Coleman Oven Corp.
    III. Robert Conte   Robert Conti
    IV. 6179846   6179846

8. I.   Grigori Schierber   Grigori Schierber   8._____
    II. Des Moines, Iowa   Des Moines, Iowa
    III. Gouverneur Hospital   Gouverneur Hospital
    IV. 91-35 Cresskill Pl.   91-35 Cresskill Pl.

9. I.   Jeffery Janssen   Jeffrey Janssen   9._____
    II. 8041071   8041071
    III. 40 Rockefeller Plaza   40 Rockafeller Plaza
    IV. 407 6 St.   406 7 St.

10. I.   5971996   5871996   10._____
    II. 3113 Knickerbocker Ave.   31123 Knickerbocker Ave.
    III. 8434 Boston Post Rd.   8424 Boston Post Rd.
    IV. Penn Station   Penn Station

Questions 11-14.

DIRECTIONS: Questions 11 through 14 are to be answered by looking at the four groups of names and addresses listed below (I, II, III, and IV), and then finding out the number of groups that have their corresponding numbered lies exactly the same.

	GROUP I	GROUP II
Line 1.	Richmond General Hospital	Richman General Hospital
Line 2.	Geriatric Clinic	Geriatric Clinic
Line 3.	3975 Paerdegat St.	3975 Peardegat St.
Line 4.	Loudonville, New York 11538	Londonville, New York 11538

	GROUP III	GROUP IV
Line 1.	Richmond General Hospital	Richmend General Hospital
Line 2.	Geriatric Clinic	Geriatric Clinic
Line 3.	3795 Paerdegat St.	3975 Paerdegat St.
Line 4.	Loudonville, New York 11358	Loudonville, New York 11538

1. In how many groups is line one exactly the same?   11._____
    A. Two   B. Three   C. Four   D. None

12. In how many groups is line two exactly the same?   12._____
    A. Two   B. Three   C. Four   D. None

13. In how many groups is line three exactly the same?   13._____
    A. Two   B. Three   C. Four   D. None

14. In how many groups is line four exactly the same? 14.____
    A. Two B. Three C. Four D. None

Questions 15-18.

DIRECTIONS: Each of Questions 15 through 18 has two lists of names and addresses. Each list contains three sets of names and addresses. Check each of the three sets in the list on the right to see if they are the same as the corresponding set in the list on the left. Mark your answers:
- A. if none of the sets in the right list are the same as those in the left list
- B. if only one of the sets in the right list is the same as those in the left list
- C. if only two of the sets in the right list are the same as those in the left list
- D. if all three sets in the right list are the same as those in the left list

15. Mary T. Berlinger
    2351 Hampton St.
    Monsey, N.Y. 20117

    Eduardo Benes
    483 Kingston Avenue
    Central Islip, N.Y. 11734

    Alan Carrington Fuchs
    17 Gnarled Hollow Road
    Los Angeles, CA 91635

    Mary T. Berlinger
    2351 Hampton St.
    Monsey, N.Y. 20117

    Eduardo Benes
    473 Kingston Avenue
    Central Islip, N.Y. 11734

    Alan Carrington Fuchs
    17 Gnarled Hollow Road
    Los Angeles, CA 91685

    15.____

16. David John Jacobson
    178 34 St. Apt. 4C
    New York, N.Y. 00927

    Ann-Marie Calonella
    7243 South Ridge Blvd.
    Bakersfield, CA 96714

    Pauline M. Thompson
    872 Linden Ave.
    Houston, Texas 70321

    David John Jacobson
    178 53 St. Apt. 4C
    New York, N.Y. 00927

    Ann-Marie Calonella
    7243 South Ridge Blvd.
    Bakersfield, CA 96714

    Pauline M. Thomson
    872 Linden Ave.
    Houston, Texas 70321

    16.____

17. Chester LeRoy Masterton
    152 Lacy Rd.
    Kankakee, Ill. 54532

    William Maloney
    S. LaCrosse Pla.
    Wausau, Wisconsin 52136

    Cynthia V. Barnes
    16 Pines Rd.
    Greenpoint, Miss. 20376

    Chester LeRoy Masterson
    152 Lacy Rd.
    Kankakee, Ill. 54532

    William Maloney
    S. LaCross Pla.
    Wausau, Wisconsin 52146

    Cynthia V. Barnes
    16 Pines Rd.
    Greenpoint,, Miss. 20376

    17.____

4 (#2)

18. Marcel Jean Frontenac   Marcel Jean Frontenac   18.____
    8 Burton On The Water   6 Burton On The Water
    Calender, Me. 01471   Calender, Me. 01471

    J. Scott Marsden   J. Scott Marsden
    174 S. Tipton St.   174 Tipton St.
    Cleveland, Ohio   Cleveland, Ohio

    Lawrence T. Haney   Lawrence T. Haney
    171 McDonough St.   171 McDonough St.
    Decatur, Ga. 31304   Decatur, Ga. 31304

Questions 19-26.

DIRECTIONS: Each of Questions 19 through 26 has two lists of numbers. Each list contains three sets of numbers. Check each of the three sets in the list on the right to see if they are the same as the corresponding set in the list on the left. Mark your answers:
    A. if none of the sets in the right list are the same as those in the left list
    B. if only one of the sets in the right list is the same as those in the left list
    C. if only two of the sets in the right list are the same as those in the left list
    D. if all three sets in the right list are the same as those in the left lists

19. 7354183476   7354983476   19.____
     4474747744   4474747774
     5791430231   57914302311

20. 7143592185   7143892185   20.____
     8344517699   8344518699
     9178531263   9178531263

21. 2572114731   257214731   21.____
     8806835476   8806835476
     8255831246   8255831246

22. 331476853821   331476858621   22.____
     6976658532996   6976655832996
     3766042113715   3766042113745

23. 8806663315   88066633115   23.____
     74477138449   74477138449
     211756663666   211756663666

24. 990006966996   99000696996   24.____
    53022219743   53022219843
    4171171117717   4171171177717

25. 24400222433004   24400222433004   25.____
    5300030055000355   5300030055500355
    20000075532002022   20000075532002022

26. 6111666406600001116   61116664066001116   26.____
    7111300117001100733   7111300117001100733
    26666446664476518   26666446664476518

Questions 27-30.

DIRECTIONS: Questions 27 through 30 are to be answered by picking the answer which is in the correct numerical order, from the lowest number to the highest number, in each question.

27. A. 44533, 44518, 44516, 44547   27.____
    B. 44516, 44518, 44533, 44547
    C. 44547, 44533, 44518, 44516
    D. 44518, 44516, 44547, 44533

28. A. 95587, 95593, 95601, 95620   28.____
    B. 95601, 95620, 95587, 95593
    C. 95593, 95587, 95601. 95620
    D. 95620, 95601, 95593, 95587

29. A. 232212, 232208, 232232, 232223   29.____
    B. 232208, 232223, 232212, 232232
    C. 232208, 232212, 232223, 232232
    D. 232223, 232232, 232208, 232208

30. A. 113419, 113521, 113462, 113462   30.____
    B. 113588, 113462, 113521, 113419
    C. 113521, 113588, 113419, 113462
    D. 113419, 113462, 113521, 113588

KEY (CORRECT ANSWERS)

1.	C	11.	A	21.	C
2.	B	12.	C	22.	A
3.	D	13.	A	23.	D
4.	A	14.	A	24.	A
5.	C	15.	C	25.	C
6.	B	16.	B	26.	C
7.	D	17.	B	27.	B
8.	A	18.	B	28.	A
9.	D	19.	B	29.	C
10.	C	20.	B	30.	D

NAME AND NUMBER COMPARISONS

COMMENTARY

This test seeks to measure your ability and disposition to do a job carefully and accurately, your attention to exactness and preciseness of detail, your alertness and versatility in discerning similarities and differences between things, and your power in systematically handling written language symbols.

It is actually a test of your ability to do academic and/or clerical work, using the basic elements of verbal (qualitative) and mathematical (quantitative) learning—words and numbers.

EXAMINATION SECTION

TEST 1

DIRECTIONS: In each line across the page there are three names or numbers that are much alike. Compare the three names or numbers and decide which ones are exactly alike. *PRINT IN THE SPACE AT THE RIGHT THE LETTER:*
    A. if all THREE names or numbers are exactly alike
    B. if only the FIRST and SECOND names or numbers are ALIKE
    C. if only the FIRST and THIRD names or numbers are alike
    D. if only the SECOND or THIRD names or numbers are alike
    E. if ALL THREE names or numbers are DIFFERENT

1. Davis Hazen   David Hozen   David Hazen   1.____
2. Lois Appel   Lois Appel   Lois Apfel   2.____
3. June Allan   Jane Allan   Jane Allan   3.____
4. 10235   10235   10235   4.____
5. 32614   32164   32614   5.____

TEST 2

1. 2395890   2395890   2395890   1.____
2. 1926341   1926347   1926314   2.____
3. E. Owens McVey   E. Owen McVey   E. Owen McVay   3.____
4. Emily Neal Rouse   Emily Neal Rowse   Emily Neal Rowse   4.____
5. H. Merritt Audubon   H. Merriott Audubon   H. Merritt Audubon   5.____

TEST 3

1. 6219354   6219354   6219354   1.____
2. 231793   2312793   2312793   2.____
3. 1065407   1065407   1065047   3.____
4. Francis Ransdell   Frances Ramsdell   Francis Ramsdell   4.____
5. Cornelius Detwiler   Cornelius Detwiler   Cornelius Detwiler   5.____

TEST 4

1. 6452054   6452564   6542054   1.____
2. 8501268   8501268   8501286   2.____
3. Ella Burk Newham   Ella Burk Newnham   Elena Burk Newnham   3.____
4. Jno. K. Ravencroft   Jno. H. Ravencroft   Jno. H. Ravencoft   4.____
5. Martin Wills Pullen   Martin Wills Pulen   Martin Wills Pullen   5.____

TEST 5

1. 3457988   3457986   3457986   1.____
2. 4695682   4695862   4695682   2.____
3. Stricklund Kaneydy   Sticklund Kanedy   Stricklund Kanedy   3.____
4. Joy Harlor Witner   Joy Harloe Witner   Joy Harloe Witner   4.____
5. R.M.O. Uberroth   R.M.O. Uberroth   R.N.O. Uberroth   5.____

TEST 6

1.	1592514	1592574	1592574	1.____
2.	2010202	2010202	2010220	2.____
3.	6177396	6177936	6177396	3.____
4.	Drusilla S. Ridgeley	Drusilla S. Ridgeley	Drusilla S. Ridgeley	4.____
5.	Andrei I. Tooumantzev	Andrei I. Tourmantzev	Andrei I. Toumantzov	5.____

TEST 7

1.	5261383	5261383	5261338	1.____
2.	8125690	8126690	8125609	2.____
3.	W.E. Johnston	W.E. Johnson	W.E. Johnson	3.____
4.	Vergil L. Muller	Vergil L. Muller	Vergil L. Muller	4.____
5.	Atherton R. Warde	Asheton R. Warde	Atherton P. Warde	5.____

TEST 8

1.	013469.5	023469.5	02346.95	1.____
2.	33376	333766	333766	2.____
3.	Ling-Temco-Vought	Ling-Tenco-Vought	Ling-Temco Vought	3.____
4.	Lorilard Corp.	Lorillard Corp.	Lorrilard Corp.	4.____
5.	American Agronomics Corporation	American Agronomics Corporation	American Agronomic Corporation	5.____

TEST 9

1.	436592864	436592864	436592864	1.____
2.	197765123	197755123	197755123	2.____
3.	Dewaay Cortvriendt International S.A.	Deway Cortvriendt International S.A.	Deway Corturiendt International S.A.	3.____
4.	Crèdit Lyonnais	Crèdit Lyonnais	Crèdit Lyonais	4.____
5.	Algemene Bank Nederland N.V.	Algamene Bank Nederland N.V.	Algemene Bank Naderland N.V.	5.____

TEST 10

1.	00032572	0.0032572	00032522	1.____
2.	399745	399745	398745	2.____
3.	Banca Privata Finanziaria S.p.A.	Banca Privata Finanzaria S.P.A.	Banca Privata Finanziaria S.P.A.	3.____
4.	Eastman Dillon, Union Securities & Co.	Eastman Dillon, Union Securities Co.	Eastman Dillon, Union Securities & Co.	4.____
5.	Arnhold and S. Bleichroeder, Inc.	Arnhold & S. Bleichroeder, Inc.	Arnold and S. Bleichroeder, Inc.	5.____

TEST 11

DIRECTIONS: Answer the questions below on the basis of the following instructions: For each such numbered set of names, addresses, and numbers listed in Columns I and II, select your answer from the following options:
A. The names in Columns I and II are different
B. The addresses in Columns I and II are different
C. The numbers in Columns I and II are different
D. The names, addresses and numbers are identical

1. Francis Jones
    62 Stately Avenue
    96-12446

    Francis Jones
    62 Stately Avenue
    96-21446

    1._____

2. Julio Montez
    19 Ponderosa Road
    56-73161

    Julio Montez
    19 Ponderosa Road
    56-71361

    2._____

3. Mary Mitchell
    2314 Melbourne Drive
    68-92172

    Mary Mitchell
    2314 Melbourne Drive
    68-92172

    3._____

4. Harry Patterson
    25 Dunne Street
    14-33430

    Harry Patterson
    25 Dunne Street
    14-34330

    4._____

5. Patrick Murphy
    171 West Hosmer Street
    93-81214

    Patrick Murphy
    171 West Hosmer Street
    93-18214

    5._____

TEST 12

1. August Schultz
816 St. Clair Avenue
53-40149

August Schultz
816 St. Claire Avenue
53-40149

1._____

2. George Taft
72 Runnymede Street
47-04033

George Taft
72 Runnymede Street
47-04023

2._____

3. Angus Henderson
1418 Madison Street
81-76375

Angus Henderson
1418 Madison Street
81-76375

3._____

4. Carolyn Mazur
12 Rivenlew Road
38-99615

Carolyn Mazur
12 Rivervane Road
38-99615

4._____

5. Adele Russell
1725 Lansing Lane
72-91962

Adela Russell
1725 Lansing Lane
72-91962

5._____

TEST 13

DIRECTIONS: The following questions are based on the instructions given below. In each of the following questions, the 3-line name and address in Column I is the master-list entry, and the 3-line entry in Column II is the information to be checked against the master list.
If there is one line that is NOT exactly alike, mark your answer A.
If there are two lines NOT exactly alike, mark your answer B.
If there are three lines NOT exactly alike, mark your answer C.
If the lines ALL are exactly alike, mark your answer D.

1. Jerome A. Jackson
   1243 14th Avenue
   New York, N.Y. 10023

   Jerome A. Johnson
   1234 14th Avenue
   New York, N.Y. 10023

   1._____

2. Sophie Strachtheim
   33-28 Connecticut Ave.
   Far Rockaway, N.Y. 11697

   Sophie Strachtheim
   33-28 Connecticut Ave.
   Far Rockaway, N.Y. 11697

   2._____

3. Elisabeth NT. Gorrell
   256 Exchange St
   New York, N.Y. 10013

   Elizabeth NT. Correll
   256 Exchange St.
   New York, N.Y. 10013

   3._____

4. Maria J. Gonzalez
   7516 E. Sheepshead Rd.
   Brooklyn, N.Y. 11240

   Maria J. Gonzalez
   7516 N. Shepshead Rd.
   Brooklyn, N.Y. 11240

   4._____

5. Leslie B. Brautenweiler
   21-57A Seller Terr.
   Flushing, N.Y. 11367

   Leslie B. Brautenwieler
   21-75ASeiler Terr.
   Flushing, N.J. 11367

   5._____

KEY (CORRECT ANSWERS)

TEST 1	TEST 2	TEST 3	TEST 4	TEST 5	TEST 6	TEST 7
1. E	1. A	1. A	1. E	1. D	1. D	1. B
2. B	2. E	2. A	2. B	2. C	2. B	2. E
3. D	3. E	3. B	3. E	3. E	3. C	3. D
4. A	4. D	4. E	4. E	4. D	4. A	4. A
5. C	5. C	5. A	5. C	5. B	5. E	5. E

TEST 8	TEST 9	TEST 10	TEST 11	TEST 12	TEST 13
1. E	1. A	1. E	1. C	1. B	1. B
2. D	2. D	2. B	2. C	2. C	2. D
3. E	3. E	3. E	3. D	3. D	3. A
4. E	4. E	4. C	4. C	4. B	4. A
5. B	5. E	5. E	5. C	5. A	5. C

NAME AND NUMBER COMPARISONS

COMMENTARY

This test seeks to measure your ability and disposition to do a job carefully and accurately, your attention to exactness and preciseness of detail, your alertness and versatility in discerning similarities and differences between things, and your power in systematically handling written language symbols.

It is actually a test of your ability to do academic and/or clerical work, using the basic elements of verbal (qualitative) and mathematical (quantitative) learning—words and numbers.

EXAMINATION SECTION

TEST 1

DIRECTIONS: Questions 1 through 6 consist of sets of names and addresses. In each question, the name and address in Column II should be an exact copy of the name and address in Column II. *PRINT IN THE SPACE AT THE RIGHT THE LETTER*
- A. if there is a mistake only in the name
- B. if there is a mistake only in the address
- C. if there is a mistake in both name and address
- D. If there is no mistake in either name or address

SAMPLE:
Michael Filbert
456 Reade Street
New York, N.Y. 10013

Michael Filbert
644 Reade Street
New York, N.Y. 10013

Since there is a mistake only in the address, the answer is B.

1. Esta Wong
   141 West 68 St.
   New York, N.Y. 10023

   Esta Wang
   141 West 68 St.
   New York, N.Y. 10023

   1.____

2. Dr. Alberto Grosso
   3475 12th Avenue
   Brooklyn, N.Y. 11218

   Dr. Alberto Grosso
   3475 12th Avenue
   Brooklyn, N.Y. 11218

   2.____

3. Mrs. Ruth Bortlas
   482 Theresa Ct.
   Far Rockaway, N.Y. 11691

   Ms. Ruth Bortias
   482 Theresa Ct.
   Far Rockaway, N.Y. 11169

   3.____

4. Mr. and Mrs. Howard Fox
   2301 Sedgwick Ave.
   Bronx, N.Y. 10468

   Mr. and Mrs. Howard Fox
   231 Sedgwick Ave.
   Bronx, N.Y. 10468

   4.____

5. Miss Marjorie Black
   223 East 23 Street
   New York, N.Y. 10010

   Miss Margorie Black
   223 East 23 Street
   New York, N.Y. 10010

   5.____

2 (#1)

6. Michelle Herman   Michelle Hermann   6._____
   806 Valley Rd.   806 Valley Dr.
   Old Tappan, N.J. 07675 Old Tappan, N.J. 07675

KEY (CORRECT ANSWERS)

1. A
2. D
3. C
4. B
5. A
6. C

TEST 2

DIRECTIONS: Questions 1 through 6 consist of sets of names and addresses. In each question, the name and address in Column II should be an exact copy of the name and address in Column II. *PRINT IN THE SPACE AT THE RIGHT THE LETTER*
- A. if there is a mistake only in the name
- B. if there is a mistake only in the address
- C. if there is a mistake in both name and address
- D. If there is no mistake in either name or address

1. Ms. Joan Kelly
   313 Franklin Ave.
   Brooklyn, N.Y. 11202

   Ms. Joan Kielly
   318 Franklin Ave.
   Brooklyn, N.Y. 11202   1.____

2. Mrs. Eileen Engel
   47-24 86 Road
   Queens, N.Y. 11122

   Mrs. Ellen Engel
   47-24 86 Road
   Queens, N.Y. 11122   2.____

3. Marcia Michaels
   213 E. 81 St.
   New York, N.Y. 10012

   Marcia Michaels
   213 E. 81 St.
   New York, N.Y. 10012   3.____

4. Rev. Edward J. Smyth
   1401 Brandeis Street
   San Francisco, Calif. 96201

   Rev. Edward J. Smyth
   1401 Brandies Street
   San Francisco, Calif. 96201   4.____

5. Alicia Rodriguez
   24-68 81 St.
   Elmhurst, N.Y. 11122

   Alicia Rodriquez
   2468 81 St.
   Elmhurst, N.Y. 11122   5.____

6. Ernest Eissemann
   21 Columbia St.
   New York, N.Y. 10007

   Ernest Eisermann
   21 Columbia St.
   New York, N.Y. 10007   6.____

KEY (CORRECT ANSWERS)

1. C
2. A
3. D
4. B
5. C
6. A

TEST 3

DIRECTIONS: Questions 1 through 8 consist of names, locations, and telephone numbers. In each question, the name, location and number in Column II should be an exact copy of the name, location, and number in Column I. *PRINT IN THE SPACE AT THE RIGHT THE LETTER*
    A. if there is a mistake in one line only
    B. if there is a mistake in two lines only
    C. if there is a mistake in three lines only
    D. if there are no mistakes in any of the lines

1. Ruth Lang
EAM Bldg., Room C101
625-2000, ext. 765

   Ruth Lang
EAM Bldg., Room C110
625-2000, ext. 765

1._____

2. Anne Marie Ionozzi
Investigations, Room 827
576-4000, ext. 832

   Anna Marie Ionozzi
Investigation, Room 827
566-4000, ext. 832

2._____

3. Willard Jameson
Fm C Bldg. Room 687
454-3010

   Willard Jamieson
Fm C Bldg. Room 687
454-3010

3._____

4. Joanne Zimmermann
Bldg. SW, Room 314
532-4601

   Joanne Zimmermann
Bldg. SW, Room 314
532-4601

4._____

5. Carlyle Whetstone
Payroll Division-A, Room 212A
262-5000, ext. 471

   Caryle Whetstone
Payroll Division-A, Room 212A
262-5000, ext. 417

5._____

6. Kenneth Chiang
Legal Council, Room 9745
(201) 416-9100, ext. 17

   Kenneth Chiang
Legal Counsel, Room 9745
(201) 416-9100, ext. 17

6._____

7. Ethel Koenig
Personnel Services Div, Rm 433
635-7572

   Ethel Hoenig
Personal Services Div, Rm 433
635-7527

7._____

8. Joyce Ehrhardt
Office of Administrator, Rm W56
387-8706

   Joyce Ehrhart
Office of Administrator, Rm W56
387-7806

8._____

2 (#3)

KEY (CORRECT ANSWERS)

1. A
2. C
3. A
4. D
5. B

6. A
7. C
8. B

TEST 4

DIRECTIONS: Each of Questions 1 through 10 gives the identification number and name of a person who has received treatment at a certain hospital. You are to choose the option (A, B, C, or D) which has EXACTLY the same number and name as those given in the question.

SAMPLE QUESTION:
123765 Frank Y. Jones
   A. 123675 Frank Y. Jones
   B. 123765 Frank T. Jones
   C. 123765 Frank Y. Jones
   D. 123765 Frank Y. Jones

The correct answer is D, because it is the only option showing the identification number and name exactly as they are in the sample question.

1. 754898 Diane Malloy
   A. 745898 Diane Malloy   B. 754898 Dion Malloy
   C. 754898 Diane Malloy   D. 754898 Diane Maloy

2. 661818 Ferdinand Figueroa
   A. 661818 Ferdinand Figeuroa   B. 661618 Ferdinand Figueroa
   C. 661818 Ferdnand Figueroa   D. 661818 Ferdinand Figueroa

3. 100101 Norman D. Braustein
   A. 100101 Norman D. Braustein   B. 101001 Norman D. Braustein
   C. 100101 Norman P. Braustien   D. 100101 Norman D. Bruastein

4. 838696 Robert Kittredge
   A. 838969 Robert Kittredge   B. 838696 Robert Kittredge
   C. 388696 Robert Kittredge   D. 838696 Robert Kittridge

5. 243716 Abraham Soletsky
   A. 243716 Abrahm Soletsky   B. 243716 Abraham Solestky
   C. 243176 Abraham Soletsky   D. 243716 Abraham Soletsky

6. 981121 Phillip M. Maas
   A. 981121 Phillip M. Mass   B. 981211 Phillip M. Maas
   C. 981121 Phillip M. Maas   D. 981121 Phillip N. Maas

7. 786556 George Macalusso
   A. 785656 George Macalusso   B. 786556 George Macalusso
   C. 786556 George Maculusso   D. 786556 George Macluasso

8. 639472 Eugene Weber
   A. 639472 Eugene Weber   B. 639472 Eugene Webre
   C. 693472 Eugene Weber   D. 639742 Eugene Weber

2 (#4)

9. 724936 John J. Lomonaco
   A. 724936 John J. Lomanoco
   B. 724396 John L. Lomonaco
   C. 7224936 John J. Lomonaco
   D. 724936 John J. Lamonaco

   9._____

10. 899868 Michael Schnitzer
    A. 899868 Micheal Schnitzer
    B. 898968 Michael Schnizter
    C. 899688 Michael Schnitzer
    D. 899868 Michael Schnitzer

    10._____

KEY (CORRECT ANSWERS)

1.	C	6.	C
2.	D	7.	B
3.	A	8.	A
4.	B	9.	C
5.	D	10.	D

NAME AND NUMBER CHECKING
EXAMINATION SECTION
TEST 1

DIRECTIONS: This test is designed to measure your speed/and accuracy. You are urged to work both quickly and accurately and to do correctly as many lists as you can in the time allowed. The test consists of lists or pairs of names and numbers. Count the number of IDENTICAL pairs in each list. Then, select the correct number, 1, 2, 3, 4, 5, and indicate your choice in the space at the right. Two sample questions are presented for your guidance, together with the correct solutions.

SAMPLE LIST A
Adelphi College – Adelphia College
Braxton Corp – Braxeton Corp.
Wassaic State School – Wassaic State School
Central Islip State Hospital – Central Isllip State Hospital
Greenwich House – Greenwich House

NOTE: There are only two correct pairs—Wassaic State School and Greenwich House. Therefore, the CORRECT answer is 2.

SAMPLE LIST B
78453694 – 78453684
784530 – 784530
533 – 534
67845 – 67845
2368745 – 2368755

NOTE: There are only two correct pairs—784530 and 67845. Therefore, the CORRECT answer is 2.

LIST 1   1.____
    Diagnostic Clinic   – Diagnostic Clinic
    Yorkville Health   – Yorkville Health
    Meinhard Clinic   – Meinhart Clinic
    Corlears Clinic   – Carlears Clinic
    Tremont Diagnostic   – Tremont Diagnostic

LIST 2   2.____
    73526   – 73526
    7283627198   – 7283627198
    627   – 637
    728352617283   – 7283526178282
    6281   – 6281

2 (#1)

LIST 3   3._____
    Jefferson Clinic — Jeffersen Clinic
    Mott Haven Center — Mott Havan Center
    Bronx Hospital — Bronx Hospital
    Montefiore Hospital — Montifeore Hospital
    Beth Isreal Hospital — Beth Israel Hospital

LIST 4   4._____
    936271826 — 936371826
    5271 — 5291
    82637192037 — 82637192037
    527182 — 5271882
    726354256 - 72635456

LIST 5   5._____
    Trinity Hospital — Trinity Hospital
    Central Harlem — Centrel Harlem
    St. Luke's Hospital — St. Lukes' Hospital
    Mt. Sinai Hospital — Mt. Sinia Hospital
    N.Y. Dispensery — N.Y. Dispensary

LIST 6   6._____
    725361552637 — 725361555637
    7526378 — 7526377
    6975 — 6975
    82637481028 — 82637481028
    3427 — 3429

LIST 7   7._____
    Misericordia Hospital — Miseracordia Hospital
    Lebonan Hospital — Lebanon Hospital
    Gouverneur Hospital — Gouverner Hospital
    German Polyclinic — German Policlinic
    French Hospital — French Hospital

LIST 8   8._____
    8277364933251 — 827364933351
    63728 — 63728
    367281 — 367281
    62733846273 — 6273846293
    62836 - 6283

LIST 9   9._____
    King's County Hospital — Kings County Hospital
    St. Johns Long Island — St. John's Long Island
    Bellevue Hospital — Bellvue Hospital
    Beth David Hospital — Beth David Hospital
    Samaritan Hospital — Samariton Hospital

3 (#1)

LIST 10   10.____
    62836454 — 62836455
    42738267 — 42738369
    573829 — 573829
    738291627874 — 738291627874
    725 - 735

LIST 11   11.____
    Bloomingdal Clinic — Bloomingdale Clinic
    Communitty Hospital — Community Hospital
    Metroplitan Hospital — Metropoliton Hospital
    Lenox Hill Hospital — Lonex Hill Hospital
    Lincoln Hospital — Lincoln Hospital

LIST 12   12.____
    6283364728 — 6283648
    627385 — 627383
    54283902 — 54283602
    63354 — 63354
    7283562781 - 7283562781

LIST 13   13.____
    Sydenham Hospital — Sydanham Hospital
    Roosevalt Hospital — Roosevelt Hospital
    Vanderbilt Clinic — Vanderbild Clinic
    Women's Hospital — Woman's Hospital
    Flushing Hospital — Flushing Hospital

LIST 14   14.____
    62738 — 62738
    727355542321 — 72735542321
    263849332 — 263849332
    262837 — 263837
    47382912 - 47382922

LIST 15   15.____
    Episcopal Hospital — Episcapal Hospital
    Flower Hospital — Flouer Hospital
    Stuyvesent Clinic — Stuyvesant Clinic
    Jamaica Clinic — Jamaica Clinic
    Ridgwood Clinic — Ridgewood Clinic

LIST 16   16.____
    628367299 — 628367399
    111 — 111
    118293304829 — 1182839489
    4448 — 4448
    333693678 - 333693678

4 (#1)

LIST 17   17.____
   Arietta Crane Farm   – Areitta Crane Farm
   Bikur Chilim Home   – Bikur Chilom Home
   Burke Foundation   – Burke Foundation
   Blythedale Home   – Blythdale Home
   Campbell Cottages   – Cambell Cottages

LIST 18   18.____
   32123   – 32132
   273893326783   – 27389326783
   473829   – 473829
   7382937   – 7383937
   3628890122332   - 36289012332

LIST 19   19.____
   Caraline Rest   – Caroline Rest
   Loreto Rest   – Loretto Rest
   Edgewater Creche   – Edgwater Creche
   Holiday Farm   – Holiday Farm
   House of St. Giles   – House of st. Giles

LIST 20   20.____
   557286777   – 55728677
   3678902   – 3678892
   1567839   – 1567839
   7865434712   – 7865344712
   9927382   - 9927382

LIST 21   21.____
   Isabella Home   – Isabela Home
   James A. Moore Home   – James A. More Home
   The Robin's Nest   – The Roben's Nest
   Pelham Home   – Pelam Home
   St. Eleanora's Home   – St. Eleanora's Home

LIST 22   22.____
   273648293048   – 273648293048
   334   – 334
   7362536478   – 7362536478
   7362819273   – 7362819273
   7362   - 7363

LIST 23   23.____
   St. Pheobe's Mission   – St. Phebe's Mission
   Seaside Home   – Seaside Home
   Speedwell Society   – Speedwell Society
   Valeria Home   – Valera Home
   Wiltwyck   - Wildwyck

5 (#1)

LIST 24
   63728   – 63738
   63728192736   – 63728192738
   428   – 458
   62738291527   – 62738291529
   63728192   - 63728192

24.____

LIST 25
   McGaffin   – McGafin
   David Ardslee   – David Ardslee
   Axton Supply   – Axeton Supply Co
   Alice Russell   – Alice Russell
   Dobson Mfg. Co. – Dobsen Mfg. Co.

25.____

KEY (CORRECT ANSWERS)

1.	3		11.	1
2.	3		12.	2
3.	1		13.	1
4.	1		14.	2
5.	1		15.	1
6.	2		16.	3
7.	1		17.	1
8.	2		18.	1
9.	1		19.	1
10.	2		20.	2

21.	1
22.	4
23.	2
24.	1
25.	2

TEST 2

DIRECTIONS: This test is designed to measure your speed/and accuracy. You are urged to work both quickly and accurately and to do correctly as many lists as you can in the time allowed. The test consists of lists or pairs of names and numbers. Count the number of IDENTICAL pairs in each list. Then, select the correct number, 1, 2, 3, 4, 5, and indicate your choice in the space at the right.

LIST 1   1._____
    82637381028   – 82637281028
    928   – 928
    72937281028   – 72937281028
    7362   – 7362
    927382615   – 927382615

LIST 2   2._____
    Albee Theatre   – Albee Theatre
    Lapland Lumber Co.   – Laplund Lumber Co.
    Adelphi College   – Adelphi College
    Jones & Son Inc.   – Jones & Sons Inc.
    S.W. Ponds Co.   – S.W. Ponds Co.

LIST 3   3._____
    85345   – 85345
    895643278   – 895643277
    726352   – 726353
    632685   – 632685
    7263524   – 7236524

LIST 4   4._____
    Eagle Library   – Eagle Library
    Dodge Ltd.   – Dodge Co.
    Stromberg Carlson   – Stromberg Carlsen
    Clairice Ling   – Clairice Linng
    Mason Book Co.   – Matson Book Co.

LIST 5   5._____
    66273   – 66273
    629   – 629
    7382517283   – 7382517283
    637281   – 639281
    2738261   – 2788261

LIST 6   6._____
    Robert MacColl   – Robert McColl
    Buick Motor   – Buck Motors
    Murray Bay & Co. Ltd.   – Murray Bay Co. Ltd.
    L.T. Ltyle   – L.T. Lyttle
    A.S. Landas   – A.S. Landas

2 (#2)

LIST 7 7.____
    6271526374890   – 627152637490
    73526189   – 73526189
    5372   – 5392
    637281142   – 63728124
    4783946   – 4783046

LIST 8 8.____
    Tyndall Burke   – Tyndell Burke
    W. Briehl   – W. Briehl
    Burritt Publishing Co.   – Buritt Publishing Co.
    Frederick Breyer & Co.   – Frederick Breyer Co.
    Bailey Buulard   – Bailey Bullard

LIST 9 9.____
    634   – 634
    16837   – 163837
    273892223678   – 27389223678
    527182   – 527782
    3628901223   – 3629002223

LIST 10 10.____
    Ernest Boas   – Ernest Boas
    Rankin Barne   – Rankin Barnes
    Edward Appley   – Edward Appely
    Camel   – Camel
    Caiger Food Co.   – Caiger Food Co.

LIST 11 11.____
    6273   – 6273
    322   – 332
    15672839   – 15672839
    63728192637   – 63728192639
    738   – 738

LIST 12 12.____
    Wells Fargo Co.   – Wells Fargo Co.
    W.D. Brett   – W.D. Britt
    Tassco Co.   – Tassko Co.
    Republic Mills   – Republic Mill
    R.W. Burnham   – R.W. Burhnam

LIST 13 13.____
    7253529152   – 7283529152
    6283   – 6383
    52839102738   – 5283910238
    308   – 398
    82637201927   – 8263720127

LIST 14
 Schumacker Co.   – Shumacker Co.
 C.H. Caiger   – C.H. Caiger
 Abraham Strauss   – Abram Straus
 B.F. Boettjer   – B.F. Boettijer
 Cut-Rate Store   – Cut-Rate Stores

14.____

LIST 15
 15273826   – 15273826
 72537   – 73537
 726391027384   – 62639107384
 637389   – 627399
 725382910   – 725382910

15.____

LIST 16
 Hixby Ltd.   – Hixby Lt'd.
 S. Reiner   – S. Riener
 Reynard Co.   – Reynord Co.
 Esso Gassoline Co.   – Esso Gasolene Co.
 Belle Brock   – Belle Brock

16.____

LIST 17
 7245   – 7245
 819263728192   – 819263728172
 682537289   – 682537298
 789   – 789
 82936542891   – 82936542891

17.____

LIST 18
 Joseph Cartwright   – Joseph Cartwrite
 Foote Food Co.   – Foot Food Co.
 Weiman & Held   – Weiman & Held
 Sanderson Shoe Co.   – Sandersen Shoe Co.
 A.M. Byrne   – A.N. Byrne

18.____

LIST 19
 4738267   – 4738277
 63728   – 63729
 6283628901   – 6283628991
 918264   – 918264
 263728192037   – 2637728192073

19.____

LIST 20
 Exray Laboratories   – Exray Labratories
 Curley Toy Co.   – Curly Toy Co.
 J. Lauer & Cross   – J. Laeur & Cross
 Mireco Brands   – Mireco Brands
 Sandor Lorand   – Sandor Larand

20.____

4 (#2)

LIST 21   21.____
   607   – 609
   6405   – 6403
   976   – 996
   101267   – 101267
   2065432   – 20965432

LIST 22   22.____
   John Macy & Sons   – John Macy & Son
   Venus Pencil Co.   – Venus Pencil Co.
   Nell McGinnis   – Nell McGinnis
   McCutcheon & Co.   – McCutcheon & Co.
   Sun-Tan Oil   – Sun-Tan Oil

LIST 23   23.____
   703345700   – 703345700
   46754   – 466754
   3367490   – 3367490
   3379   – 3778
   47384   – 47394

LIST 24   24.____
   arthritis   – arthritis
   asthma   – asthma
   endocrine   – endocrene
   gastro-enterological – gastrol-enteralogical
   orthopedic   – orthopedic

LIST 25   25.____
   743829432   – 743828432
   998   – 998
   732816253902   – 732816252902
   46829   – 46830
   7439120249   – 7439210249

KEY (CORRECT ANSWERS)

1.	4	11.	3
2.	3	12.	1
3.	2	13.	1
4.	1	14.	1
5.	2	15.	2
6.	1	16.	1
7.	2	17.	3
8.	1	18.	1
9.	1	19.	1
10.	3	20.	1

21. 1
22. 4
23. 2
24. 3
25. 1

NAME AND NUMBER CHECKING
EXAMINATION SECTION
TEST 1

DIRECTIONS: This test is designed to measure your speed/and accuracy. You are urged to work both quickly and accurately and to do correctly as many lists as you can in the time allowed. The test consists of lists or pairs of names and numbers. Count the number of IDENTICAL pairs in each list. Then, select the correct number, 1, 2, 3, 4, 5, and indicate your choice in the space at the right. Two sample questions are presented for your guidance, together with the correct solutions.

<u>SAMPLE LIST A</u>
Adelphi College — Adelphia College
Braxton Corp — Braxeton Corp.
Wassaic State School — Wassaic State School
Central Islip State Hospital — Central Isllip State Hospital
Greenwich House — Greenwich House

NOTE: There are only two correct pairs—Wassaic State School and Greenwich House. Therefore, the CORRECT answer is 2.

<u>SAMPLE LIST B</u>
78453694 — 78453684
784530 — 784530
533 — 534
67845 — 67845
2368745 — 2368755

NOTE: There are only two correct pairs—784530 and 67845. Therefore, the CORRECT answer is 2.

LIST 1   1._____
    98654327 — 98654327
    74932564 — 7492564
    61438652 — 61438652
    01297653 — 01287653
    1865439765 — 1865439765

LIST 2   2._____
    478362 — 478363
    278354792 — 278354772
    9327 — 9327
    297384625 — 27384625
    6428156 — 6428158

2 (#1)

LIST 3   3.____
    Abbey House   - Abbey House
    Actor's Fund Home   - Actor's Fund Home
    Adrian Memorial   - Adrian Memorial
    A. Clayton Powell Home   - Clayton Powell House
    Abbot E. Kittredge Club   - Abbott E. Kitteredge Club

LIST 4   4.____
    3682   - 3692
    21937453829   - 31927453829
    723   - 733
    2763920   - 2763920
    47293   - 47293

LIST 5   5.____
    Adra House   - Adra House
    Adolescents' Court   - Adolescents' Court
    Cliff Villa   - Cliff Villa
    Clark Neighborhood House   - Clark Neighborhood House
    Alma Mathews House   - Alma Mathews House

LIST 6   6.____
    28734291   - 28734271
    63810263849   - 63810263846
    26831027   - 26831027
    368291   - 368291
    7238102637   - 7238102637

LIST 7   7.____
    Albion State T.S.   - Albion State T.C.
    Clara de Hirsch Home   - Clara De Hirsch Home
    Alice Carrington Royce   - Alice Carington Royce
    Alice Chopin Nursery   - Alice Chapin Nursery
    Lighthouse Eye Clinic   - Lighthouse Eye Clinic

LIST 8   8.____
    327   - 329
    712438291026   - 712438291026
    2753829142   - 275382942
    826287   - 826289
    26435162839   - 26435162839

LIST 9   9.____
    Letchworth Village   - Letchworth Village
    A.A.A.E. Inc.   - A.A.A.E. Inc.
    Clear Pool Camp   - Clear Pool Camp
    A.M.M.L.A. Inc.   - A.M.M.L.A. Inc.
    J.G. Harbard   - J.G. Harbord

3 (#1)

LIST 10   10.____
    8254   - 8256
    2641526   - 2641526
    4126389012   - 4126389102
    725   - 725
    76253917287   - 76253917287

LIST 11   11.____
    Attica State Prison   - Attica State Prison
    Nellie Murrah   - Nellie Murrah
    Club Marshall   - Club Marshal
    Assissium Casea-Maria - Assissium Casa-Maria
    The Homestead   - The Homestead

LIST 12   12.____
    2691   - 2691
    623819253627   - 623819253629
    28637   - 28937
    278392736   - 278392736
    52739   - 52739

LIST 13   13.____
    A.I.C.P. Boys Camp   - A.I.C.P. Boy's Camp
    Einar Chrystie   - Einar Christyie
    Astoria Center   - Astoria Center
    G. Frederick Brown   - G. Federick Browne
    Vacation Service   - Vacation Services

LIST 14   14.____
    728352689   - 728352688
    643728   - 643728
    37829176   - 37827196
    8425367   - 8425369
    65382018   - 65382018

LIST 15   15.____
    E.S. Streim   - E.S. Strim
    Charles E. Higgins   - Charles E. Higgins
    Baluvelt, N.Y.   - Blauwelt, N.Y.
    Roberta Magdalen   - Roberto Magdalen
    Ballard School   - Ballard School

LIST 16   16.____
    7382   - 7392
    281374538299   - 291374538299
    623   - 633
    6273730   - 6273730
    63392   - 63392

4 (#1)

LIST 17
    Orrin Otis — Orrin Otis
    Barat Settlement — Barat Settlemen
    Emmanuel House — Emmanuel House
    William T. McCreery — William T. McCreery
    Seamen's Home — Seaman's Home

17._____

LIST 18
    72824391 — 72834371
    3729106237 — 37291106237
    82620163849 — 82620163846
    37638921 — 37638921
    82631027 — 82631027

18._____

LIST 19
    Commonwealth Fund — Commonwealth Fund
    Anne Johnsen — Anne Johnson
    Bide-A-Wee Home — Bide-a-Wee Home
    Riverdale-on-Hudson — Riverdal-on-Hudson
    Bialystoker Home — Bailystoker Home

19._____

LIST 20
    9271 — 9271
    392918352627 — 392018852629
    72637 — 72637
    927392736 — 927392736
    92739 — 92739

20._____

LIST 21
    Charles M. Stump — Charles M. Stump
    Bourne Workshop — Buorne Workshop
    B'nai Bi'rith — B'nai Brith
    Poppenhuesen Institute — Poppenheusen Institute
    Consular Service — Consular Service

21._____

LIST 22
    927352689 — 927352688
    647382 — 648382
    93729176 — 93727196
    649536718 — 649536718
    5835367 — 5835369

22._____

LIST 23
    L.S. Bestend — L.S. Bestent
    Hirsch Mfg. Co. — Hircsh Mfg. Co.
    F.H. Storrs — F.P. Storrs
    Camp Wassaic — Camp Wassaic
    George Ballingham — George Ballingham

23._____

5 (#1)

LIST 24 24.____
  372846392048 - 372846392048
  334 - 334
  7283524678 - 7283524678
  7283 - 7283
  7283629372 - 7283629372

LIST 25 25.____
  Dr. Stiles Company - Dr. Stills Company
  Frances Hunsdon - Frances Hunsdon
  Northrop Barrert - Nothrup Barrent
  J.D. Brunjes - J.D. Brunjes
  Theo. Claudel & Co. - Theo. Claudel co.

KEY (CORRECT ANSWERS)

1.	3		11.	3
2.	1		12.	3
3.	2		13.	1
4.	2		14.	2
5.	5		15.	2
6.	3		16.	2
7.	1		17.	3
8.	2		18.	2
9.	4		19.	2
10.	3		20.	4

21. 2
22. 1
23. 2
24. 5
25. 2

TEST 2

DIRECTIONS: This test is designed to measure your speed/and accuracy. You are urged to work both quickly and accurately and to do correctly as many lists as you can in the time allowed. The test consists of lists or pairs of names and numbers. Count the number of IDENTICAL pairs in each list. Then, select the correct number, 1, 2, 3, 4, 5, and indicate your choice in the space at the right.

LIST 1   1.____
    82728   - 82738
    82736292637   - 82736292639
    728   - 738
    83926192527   - 83726192529
    82736272   - 82736272

LIST 2   2.____
    L. Pietri   - L. Pietri
    Mathewson, L.F.   - Mathewson, L.F.
    Funk & Wagnall   - Funk & Wagnalls
    Shimizu, Sojio   - Shimizu, Sojio
    Filing Equipment Bureau - Filing Equipment Buraeu

LIST 3   3.____
    63801829374   - 63801839474
    283577657   - 283577657
    65689   - 65689
    3457892026   - 3547893026
    2779   - 2778

LIST 4   4.____
    August Caille   - August Caille
    The Well-Fare Service   - The Wel-Fare Service
    K.L.M. Process co.   - R.L.M. Process Co.
    Merrill Littell   - Merrill Littell
    Dodd & Sons   - Dodd & Son

LIST 5   5.____
    998745732   - 998745733
    723   - 723
    463849102983   - 463849102983
    8570   - 8570
    279012   - 279012

LIST 6   6.____
    M.A. Wender   - M.A. Winder
    Minneapolis Supply Co.   - Minneapolis Supply Co.
    Beverly Hills Corp   - Beverley Hills Corp.
    Trafalgar Square   - Trafalgar Square
    Phifer, D.T.   - Phiefer, D.T.

2 (#2)

LIST 7
   7834629   - 7834629
   3549806746   - 3549806746
   97802564   - 97892564
   689246   - 688246
   2578024683   - 2578024683

7.____

LIST 8
   Scadrons'   - Scadrons'
   Gensen & Bro.   - Genson & Bro.
   Firestone Co.   - Firestone Co.
   H.L. Eklund   - H.L. Eklund
   Oleomargarine Co.   - Oleomargarine Co.

8.____

LIST 9
   782039485618   - 782039485618
   53829172639   - 63829172639
   892   - 892
   82937482   - 829374820
   52937456   - 53937456

9.____

LIST 10
   First Nat'l Bank   - First Nat'l Bank
   Sedgwick Machine Works - Sedgewick Machine Works
   Hectographia Co.   - Hectographia Corp.
   Levet Bros.   - Levet Bros.
   Multistamp Co., Inc. - Multistamp Co., Inc.

10.____

LIST 11
   7293   - 7293
   6382910293   - 6382910292
   981928374012   - 981928374912
   58293   - 58393
   18203649271   - 283019283745

11.____

LIST 12
   Lowrey Lb'r Co.   - Lowrey Lb'r Co.
   Fidelity Service   - Fidelity Service
   Reumann, J.A.   - Reumann, J.A.
   Duophoto Ltd.   - Duophotos Ltd.
   John Jarratt   - John Jaratt

12.____

LIST 13
   6820384   - 6820384
   383019283745   - 383019283745
   63927102   - 63928102
   91029354829   - 91029354829
   58291728   - 58291728

13.____

3 (#2)

LIST 14 14.____
    Standard Press Co.   - Standard Press Co.
    Reliant Mf'g. Co.   - Relant Mf'g Co.
    M.C. Lynn   - M.C. Lynn
    J. Fredericks Company   - G. Fredericks Company
    Wandermann, B.S.   - Wanderman, B.S.

LIST 15 15.____
    4283910293   - 4283010203
    992018273648   - 992018273848
    620   - 629
    752937273   - 752937373
    5392   - 5392

LIST 16 16.____
    Waldorf Hotel   - Waldorf Hotel
    Aaron Machinery Co.   - Aaron Machinery Co.
    Caroline Ann Locke   - Caroline Ane Locke
    McCabe Mfg. Co.   - McCabe Mfg. Co.
    R.L. Landres   - R.L. Landers

LIST 17 17.____
    68391028364   - 68391028394
    68293   - 68293
    739201   - 739201
    72839201   - 72839211
    739917   - 739719

LIST 18 18.____
    Balsam M.M.   - Balsamm, M.M.
    Steinway & Co.   - Stienway & M. Co.
    Eugene Elliott   - Eugene A. Elliott
    Leonard Loan Co.   - Leonard Loan Co.
    Frederick Morgan   - Frederick Morgen

LIST 19 19.____
    8929   - 9820
    392836472829   - 392836572829
    462   - 4622039271
    827   - 2039276837
    53829   - 54829

LIST 20 20.____
    Danielson's Hofbrau   - Danielson's Hafbrau
    Edward A. Truarme   - Edward A. Truame
    Insulite Co.   - Insulite Co.
    Reisler Shoe Corp.   - Rielser Shoe Corp.
    L.L. Thompson   - L.L. Thompson

4 (#2)

LIST 21 21.____
   92839102837 - 92839102837
   58891028 - 58891028
   7291728 - 7291928
   272839102839 - 272839102839
   428192 - 428102

LIST 22 22.____
   K.L. Veiller - K.L. Veiller
   Webster, Roy - Webster, Ray
   Drasner Spring Co. - Drasner Spring Co.
   Edward J. Cravenport - Edward J. Cravanport
   Harold Field - Harold A. Field

LIST 23 23.____
   2293 - 2293
   4283910293 - 5382910292
   871928374012 - 871928374912
   68293 - 68393
   8120364927 - 81293649271

LIST 24 24.____
   Tappe, Inc - Tappe, Inc.
   A.M. Wentingworth - A.M. Wentinworth
   Scott A. Elliott - Scott A. Elliott
   Echeverria Corp. - Echeverria Corp.
   Bradford Victor Company - Bradford Victer Company

LIST 25 25.____
   4820384 - 4820384
   393019283745 - 283919283745
   63917102 - 63927102
   91029354829 - 91029354829
   48291728 - 48291728

KEY (CORRECT ANSWERS)

1.	1	11.	1
2.	3	12.	3
3.	2	13.	4
4.	2	14.	2
5.	4	15.	1
6.	2	16.	3
7.	3	17.	2
8.	4	18.	1
9.	2	19.	1
10.	3	20.	2

21. 3
22. 2
23. 1
24. 2
25. 4

BASIC FUNDAMENTALS OF FILING SCIENCE

TABLE OF CONTENTS

	Page
I. COMMENTARY	1
II. BASICS OF FILING	1
1. Types of Files	1
a. Shannon File	1
b. Spindle File	1
c. Box File	1
d. Flat File	1
e. Bellows File	1
f. Vertical File	1
g. Clip File	1
h. Visible File	2
i. Rotary File	2
2. Aids in Filing	2
3. Variations of Filing Systems	2
4. Centralized Filing	2
5. Methods of Filing	3
a. Alphabetic Filing	3
b. Subject Filing	3
c. Geographical Filing	3
d. Chronological Filing	3
e. Numerical Filing	3
6. Indexing	3
7. Alphabetizing	4
III. RULES FOR INDEXING AND ALPHABETIZING	4
IV. OFFICIAL EXAMINATION DIRECTIONS AND RULES	8
1. Official Directions	8
2. Official Rules For Alphabetical Filing	9
a. Names of Individuals	9
b. Names of Business Organizations	9
3. Sample Question	9

BASIC FUNDAMENTALS OF FILING SCIENCE

I. COMMENTARY

Filing is the systematic arrangement and storage of papers, cards, forms, catalogues, etc. so that they may be found easily and quickly. The importance of an efficient filing system cannot be emphasized too strongly. The filed materials form records which may be needed quickly to settle questions that may cause embarrassing situations if such evidence is not available. In addition to keeping papers in order so that they are readily available, the filing system must also be designed to keep papers in good condition. A filing system must be planned so that papers may be filed easily, withdrawn easily, and as quickly returned to their proper place. The cost of a filing system is also an important factor

The need for a filing system arose when the businessman began to carry on negotiations on a large scale. He could no longer be intimate with the details of his business. What was needed in the early era was a spindle or pigeon-hole desk. Filing in pigeon-hole desks is now almost completely extinct. It was an unsatisfactory practice since pigeon holes were not labeled, and the desk was an untidy mess.

II. BASIS OF FILING

The science of filing is an exact one and entails a thorough understanding of basic facts, materials, and methods. An overview of this important information now follows.

1. Types of Files

    a. Shannon File: This consists of a board, at one end of which are fastened two arches which may be opened laterally.

    b. Spindle File: This consists of a metal or wood base to which is attached a long, pointed spike. Papers are pushed down on the spike as received. This file is useful for temporary retention of papers.

    c. Box File: This is a heavy cardboard or metal box, opening from the side like a book.

    d. Flat File: This consists of a series of shallow drawers or trays, arranged like drawers in a cabinet.

    e. Bellows File: This is a heavy cardboard container with alphabetized or compartment sections, the ends of which are enclosed in such a manner that they resemble an accordion.

    f. Vertical File: This consists of one or more drawers in which the papers are stood on edge, usually in folders, and are indexed by guides. A series of two or more drawers in one unit is the usual file cabinet.

    g. Clip File: This file has a large clip attached to a board and is very similar to the Shannon File.

h. Visible File: Cards are filed flat in an overlapping arrangement which leaves a part of each card visible at all times.

i. Rotary File: The rotary file has a number of visible card files attached to a post around which they can be revolved. The wheel file has visible cards which rotate around a horizontal axis.

j. Tickler File: This consists of cards or folders marked with the days of the month, in which materials are filed and turned up on the appropriate day of the month.

2. Aids in Filing

a. Guides: Guides are heavy cardboard, pasteboard, or Bristol-board sheets the same size as folders. At the top is a tab on which is marked or printed the distinguishing letter, words, or numbers indicating the material filed in a section of the drawer.

b. Sorting Trays: Sorting trays are equipped with alphabetical guides to facilitate the sorting of papers preparatory to placing them in a file.

c. Coding: Once the classification or indexing caption has been determined, it must be indicated on the letter for filing purposes.

d. Cross-Reference: Some letters or papers might easily be called for under two or more captions. For this purpose, a cross-reference card or sheet is placed in the folder or in the index.

3. Variations of Filing Systems

a. Variadex Alphabetic Index: Provides for more effective expansion of the alphabetic system.

b. Triple-Check Numeric Filing: Entails a multiple cross-reference, as the name implies.

c. Variadex Filing: Makes use of color as an aid in filing.

d. Dewey Decimal System: The system is a numeric one used in libraries or for filing library materials in an office. This special type of filing system is used where material is grouped in finely divided categories, such as in libraries. With this method, all material to be filed is divided into ten major groups, from 000 to 900, and then subdivided into tens, units, and decimals.

4. Centralized Filing

Centralized filing means keeping the files in one specific or central location. Decentralized filing means putting away papers in files of individual departments. The first step in the organization of a central filing department is to make a careful canvass of all desks in the offices. In this manner we can determine just what material needs to be filed, and what information each desk occupant requires from the central file. Only papers which may be used at some time by persons in the various offices should be placed in the central file. A paper that is to be used at some time by persons in the various offices should be placed in the central file. A paper that is to be used by one department only should never be filed in the central file.

5. Methods of Filing

   While there are various methods used for filing, actually there are only five basic systems: alphabetical, subject, numerical, geographic, and chronological. All other systems are derived from one of these or from a combination of two or more of them. Since the purpose of a filing system is to store business records systemically so that any particular record can be found almost instantly when required, filing requires, in addition to the proper kinds of equipment and supplies, an effective method of indexing.
   There are five basic systems of filing:

   a. Alphabetic Filing: Most filing is alphabetical. Other methods, as described below, require extensive alphabetization. In alphabetical filing, lettered dividers or guides are arranged in alphabetic sequence. Material to be filed is placed behind the proper guide. All materials under each letter are also arranged alphabetically. Folders are used unless the file is a card index.

   b. Subject Filing: This method is used when a single, complete file on a certain subject is desired. A subject file is often maintained to assemble all correspondence on a certain subject. Such files are valuable in connection with insurance claims, contract negotiations, personnel, and other investigations, special programs, and similar subjects.

   c. Geographical File: Materials are filed according to location: states, cities, counties, or other subdivisions. Statistics and tax information are often filed in this manner.

   d. Chronological File: Records are filed according to date. This method is used especially in "tickler" files that have guides numbered 1 to 31 for each day of the month. Each number indicates the day of the month when the filed item requires attention.

   e. Numerical File: This method requires an alphabetic card index giving name and number. The card index is used to locate records numbered consecutively in the files according to date received or sequence in which issued, such as licenses, permits, etc.

6. Indexing

   Determining the name or title under which an item is to be filed is known as indexing. For example, how would a letter from Robert E. Smith be filed? The name would be rearranged Smith, Robert E., so that the letter would be filed under the last name.

7. Alphabetizing

The arranging of names for filing is known as alphabetizing. For example, suppose you have four letters indexed under the names Johnson, Becker, Roe, and Stern. How should these letters be arranged in the files so that they may be found easily? You would arrange the four names alphabetically, thus Becker, Johnson, Roe, and Stern.

III. RULES FOR INDEXING AND ALPHABETIZING

1. The names of persons are to be transposed. Write the surname first, then the given name, and, finally, the middle name or initial. Then arrange the various names according to the alphabetic order of letters throughout the entire name. If there is a title, consider that after the middle name or initial.

NAMES	INDEXED AS
Arthur L. Bright	Bright, Arthur L.
Arthur S. Bright	Bright, Arthur S.
P.E. Cole	Cole, P.E.
Dr. John C. Fox	Fox, John C. (Dr.)

2. If a surname includes the same letters of another surname, with one or more additional letters added to the end, the shorter surname is placed first regardless of the given name or the initial of the given name.

NAMES	INDEXED AS
Robert E. Brown	Brown, Robert E.
Gerald A. Browne	Browne, Gerald A.
William O. Brownell	Brownell, William O.

3. Firm names are alphabetized under the surnames. Words like the, an, a, of, and for, are not considered.

NAMES	INDEXED AS
Bank of America	Bank of America
Bank Discount Dept.	Bank Discount Dept.
The Cranford Press	Cranford Press, The
Nelson Dwyer & Co.	Dwyer, Nelson, & Co.
Sears, Roebuck & Co.	Sears Roebuck & Co.
Montgomery Ward & Co.	Ward, Montgomery, & Co.

4. The order of filing is determined first of all by the first letter of the names to be filed. If the first letters are the same, the order is determined by the second letters, and so on. In the following pairs of names, the order is determined by the letters underlined:

   | A__u__sten | H__a__yes | Ha__n__son | Har__v__ey | Heat__h__ | Gree__n__ | Schwa__r__tz |
   | Baker | H__e__ath | Ha__r__per | Har__w__ood | Hea__t__on | Gree__n__e | Schwa__r__z |

   A__u__sten H__a__yes Ha__n__son Har__v__ey Heat__h__ Gree__n__ Schwar__t__z
   B__a__ker   H__e__ath Ha__r__per Har__w__ood Hea__t__on Gree__n__e Schwar__z__

5. When surnames are alike, those with initials only precede those with given names, unless the first initial comes alphabetically after the first letter of the name.

Gleason, S.	*but*, Abbott, Mary
Gleason, S.W.	Abbott, W.B.
Gleason, Sidney	

6. Hyphenated names are treated as if spelled without the hyphen.
    Lloyd, Paul N.   Lloyd, Robert
    Lloyd-Jones, James   Lloyd-Thomas, A.S.

7. Company names composed of single letters which are not used as abbreviations precede the other names beginning with the same letter.
    B & S Garage   E Z Duplicator Co.
    B X Cable Co.   Eagle Typewriter Co.
    Babbitt, R.N.   Edison Company

8. The ampersand (&) and the apostrophe (') in firm names are disregarded in alphabetizing.
    Nelson & Niller   M & C Amusement Corp.
    Nelson, Walter J.   M C Art Assn.
    Nelson's Bakery

9. Names beginning with Mac, Mc, or M' are usually placed in regular order as spelled. Some filing systems file separately names beginning with Mc.
    MacDonald, R.J.   Mazza, Anthony
    MacDonald, S.B.   McAdam, Wm.
    Mace, Wm.   McAndrews, Jerry

10. Names beginning with St. are listed as if the name Saint were spelled in full. Numbered street names and all abbreviated names are treated as if spelled out in full.
    Saginaw   Fifth Avenue Hotel   Hart Mfg. Co.
    St. Louis   42nd Street Dress Shop   Hart, Martin
    St. Peter's Rectory Hart, Chas.   Hart, Thos.
    Sandford   Hart, Charlotte   Hart, Thomas A.
    Smith, Wm.   Hart, Jas.   Hart, Thos. R.
    Smith, Willis   Hart, Janice

11. Federal, state, or city departments of government should be placed alphabetically under the governmental branch controlling them.
    Illinois, State of – Departments and Commissions
        Banking Dept.
        Employment Bureau
    United States Government Departments
        Commerce
        Defense
        State
        Treasury

12. Alphabetic Order: Each word in a name is an indexing unit. Arrange the names in alphabetic order by comparing similar units in each name. Consider the second units only when the first units are identical. Consider the third units only when both the first and second units are identical.

13. Single Surnames or Initials: A surname, when used alone, precedes the same surname with a first name or initial. A surname with a first initial only precedes a surname with a complete first name. This rule is sometimes stated, "nothing comes before something."

14. Surname Prefixes: A surname prefix is not a separate indexing unit, but it is considered part of the surname. These prefixes include: d', D', Da, de, De, Del, Des, Di, Du, Fitz., La, Le, Mc, Mac, 'c, O', St., Van, Van der, Von, Von der, and others. The prefixes M', Mac, and Mc are indexed and filed exactly as they are spelled.

15. Names of Firms: Names of firms and institutions are indexed and filed exactly as they are written when they do not contain the complete name of an individual.

16. Names of Firms Containing Complete Individual Names: When the firm or institution name includes the complete name of an individual, the units are transposed for indexing in the same way as the name of an individual.

17. Article "The": When the article "the" occurs at the beginning of a name, it is placed at the end in parentheses but it is not moved. In both cases, it is not an indexing unit and is disregarded in filing.

18. Hyphenated Names: Hyphenated firm names are considered as separate indexing units. Hyphenated surnames of individuals are considered as one indexing unit; this applies also to hyphenated names of individuals whose complete names are part of a firm name.

19. Abbreviations: Abbreviations are considered as though the name were written in full; however, single letters other than abbreviations are considered as separate indexing units.

20. Conjunctions, Prepositions, and Firm Endings: Conjunctions and prepositions, such as and, for, in, of, are disregarded in indexing and filing but are not omitted or their order changed when writing names on cards and folders. Firm endings, such as Ltd., Inc., So., Son, Bros., Mfg., and Corp. , are treated as a unit in indexing and filing and are considered as though spelled in full, such as Brothers and Incorporated.

21. One of Two Words: Names that may be spelled either as one or two words are indexed and filed as one word.

22. Compound Geographic Names: Compound geographic names are considered as separate indexing and filing units, except when the first part of the name is not an English word, such as the Los in Los Angeles.

23. Titles or degrees of individuals, whether preceding or following the name, are not considered in indexing or filing. They are placed in parentheses after the given name or initial. Terms that designate seniority, such as Jr., Sr., 2d, are also placed in parentheses and are considered for indexing and filing only when the names to be indexed are otherwise identical.

Exception A: When the name of an individual consists of a title and one name only, such as Queen Elizabeth, it is not transposed and the title is considered for indexing and filing.

Exception B: When a title or foreign article is the initial word of a firm or association name, it is considered for indexing and filing.

24. Possessives: When a word ends in apostrophe s, the s is not considered in indexing and filing. However, when a word ends in s apostrophe, because the s is part of the original word, it is considered. This rule is sometimes stated, "Consider everything up to the apostrophe."

25. United States and Foreign Government Names: Names pertaining to the federal government are indexed and filed under United States Government and then subdivided by title of the department, bureau, division, commission, or board. Names pertaining to foreign governments are indexed and filed under names of countries and then subdivided by title of the department, bureau, division, commission, or board. Phrases, such as department of, bureau of, division of, commission of, board of, when used in titles of governmental bodies, are placed in parentheses after the word they modify, but are disregarded in indexing and filing. Such phrases, however, are considered in indexing and filing governmental names.

26. Other Political Subdivisions: Names pertaining to other political subdivisions, such as states, counties, cities, or towns, are indexed and filed under the name of the political subdivision and then subdivided by the title of the department, bureau, division, commission, or board.

27. When the same name appears with different addresses, the names are indexed as usual and arranged alphabetically according to city or town. The State is considered only when there is duplication of both individual or company name and city name. If the same name is located at different addresses within the same city, then the names are arranged alphabetically by streets. If the same name is located at more than one address on the same street then the names are arranged from the lower to the higher street number.

28. Numbers: Any number in a name is considered as though it were written in words, and it is indexed and filed as one unit.

29. Bank Names: Because the names of many banking institutions are alike in several respects, as First National Bank, Second National Bank, etc., banks are indexed and filed first by city location, then by bank name, with the state location written in parentheses and considered only if necessary.

30. Married Women: The legal name of a married woman is the one used for filing purposes. Legally, a man's surname is the only part of a man's name a woman assumes when she marries. Her legal name, therefore, could be either:
    a. Her own first and middle names together with her husband's surname, or
    b. Her own first name and maiden surname, together with her husband's surname.

Mrs. is placed in parentheses at the end of the name. Her husband's first and middle names are given in parentheses below her legal name.

31. An alphabetically arranged list of names illustrating many difficult points of alphabetizing follows:

COLUMN I	COLUMN II
Abbot, W.B.	54th St. Tailor Shop
Abbot, Alice	Forstall, W.J.
Allen Alexander B.	44th St. Garage
Allen, Alexander B., Inc.	M A Delivery Co.
Andersen, Hans	M & C Amusement Corp.
Andersen, Hans E.	M C Art Assn.
Andersen, Hans E., Jr.	MacAdam, Wm.
Anderson, Andrew Andrews,	Macaulay, James
George Brown Motor Co., Boston	MacAulay, Wilson
Brown Motor Co., Chicago	MacDonald, R.J.
Brown Motor Co., Philadelphia	Macdonald, S. B.
Brown Motor Co., San Francisco	Mace, Wm.
Dean, Anna	Mazza, Anthony
Dean, Anna F.	McAdam, Wm.
Dean, Anna Frances	McAndrews, Jerry
Dean & Co.	Meade & Clark Co.
Deane-Arnold Apartments	Meade, S.T.
Deane's Pharmacy	Meade, Soloman
Deans, Felix A.	Sackett Publishing Co.
Dean's Studio	Sacks, Robert
Deans, Wm.	St. Andrew Hotel
Deans & Williams	St. John, Homer W.
East Randolph	Saks, Isaac B.
East St. Louis	Stephens, Ira
Easton, Pa.	Stevens, Delevan
Eastport, Me.	Stevens, Delila

IV. OFFICIAL EXAMINATION DIRECTIONS AND RULES

To preclude the possibility of conflicting or varying methods of filing, explicit directions and express rules are given to the candidate before he answers the filing questions on an examination.

The most recent official directions and rules for the filing questions are given immediately hereafter.

OFFICIAL DIRECTIONS

Each of questions…to…consists of four (five) names. For each question, select the one of the four(five) names that should be first (second)(third)(last) if the four (five(names were arranged in alphabetical order in accordance with the rules for alphabetical filing given below. Read these rules carefully. Then, for each question, indicate in the correspondingly numbered row on the answer sheet the letter preceding the name that should be first(second)(third)(last) in alphabetical order.

OFFICIAL RULES FOR ALPHABETICAL FILING

Names of Individuals

1. The names of individuals are filed in strict alphabetical order, first according to the last name, then according to first name or initial, and, finally, according to middle name or initial. For example: William Jones precedes George Kirk and Arthur S. Blake precedes Charles M. Blake.
2. When the last names are identical, the one with an initial instead of a first name precedes the one "with a first name beginning with the same initial." For example: J. Green precedes Joseph Green.
3. When identical last names also have identical first names, the one without a middle name or initial precedes the one with a middle name or initial. For example: Robert Jackson precedes both Robert C. Jackson and Robert Chester Jackson.
4. When last names are identical and the first names are also identical, the one with a middle initial precedes the one with a middle name beginning with the same initial. For example: Peter A. Brown precedes Peter Alvin Brown.
5. Prefixes such as De, El, La, and Van are considered parts of the names they precede. For example: Wilfred DeWald precedes Alexander Duval.
6. Last names beginning with "Mac" or "Mc" are filed as spelled.
7. Abbreviated names are treated as if they were spelled out. For example: Jos. is filed as Joseph and Robt. is filed as Robert.
8. Titles and designations such as Dr., Mrs., Prof. are disregarding in filing.

Names of Business Organizations

1. The names of business organizations are filed exactly as written, except that an organization bearing the name of an individual is filed alphabetically according to the name of the individual in accordance with the rules for filing names of individuals given above. For example: Thomas Allison Machine Company precedes Northern Baking Company.
2. When numerals occur in a name, they are treated as if they were spelled out. For example: 6 stands for six and 4th stands for fourth.
3. When the following words occur in names, they are disregarded: the, of

SAMPLE QUESTION

Choose the name that should be filed third.
A. Fred Town (2)   B. Jack Towne (3)   C. D. Town (1)   D. Jack Stone (4)
The numbers in parentheses indicate the proper alphabetical order in which these names should be filed. Since the name that should be filed <u>third</u> is Jack Towne, the answer is (B).

FILING
EXAMINATION SECTION
TEST 1

DIRECTIONS: Each of the following questions contains four names. For each question, choose the name that should be FIRST if the four names are to be arranged in alphabetical order in accordance with the Rules for Alphabetical Filing given before. Read these rules carefully. Then, for each question, indicate in the space at the right the letter before the name that should be FIRST in alphabetical order.

    SAMPLE QUESTION
    A. Jane Earl   (2)
    B. James A. Earle   (4)
    C. James Earl   (1)
    D. J. Earle   (3)

The numbers in parentheses show the proper alphabetical order in which these names should be filed. Since the name that should be filed FIRST is James Earl, the answer to the Sample Question is C.

1. A. Majorca Leather Goods   B. Robert Maiorca and Sons   1.____
   C. Maintenance Management Corp.   D. Majestic Carpet Mills

2. A. Municipal Telephone Service   B. Municipal Reference Library   2.____
   C. Municipal Credit Union   D. Municipal Broadcasting System

3. A. Robert B. Pierce   B. R. Bruce Pierce   3.____
   C. Ronald Pierce   D. Robert Bruce Pierce

4. A. Four Seasons Sports Club   B. 14 Street Shopping Center   4.____
   C. Forty Thieves Restaurant   D. 42nd St. Theaters

5. A. Franco Franceschini   B. Amos Franchini   5.____
   C. Sandra Franceschia   D. Lilie Franchinesca

KEY (CORRECT ANSWERS)

1. C
2. D
3. B
4. D
5. C

TEST 2

DIRECTIONS: Each of the following questions contains four names. For each question, choose the name that should be FIRST if the four names are to be arranged in alphabetical order in accordance with the Rules for Alphabetical Filing given before. Read these rules carefully. Then, for each question, indicate in the space at the right the letter before the name that should be FIRST in alphabetical order.

    SAMPLE QUESTION
    A. Jane Earl   (2)
    B. James A. Earle (4)
    C. James Earl   (1)
    D. J. Earle   (3)

The numbers in parentheses show the proper alphabetical order in which these names should be filed. Since the name that should be filed FIRST is James Earl, the answer to the Sample Question is C.

1. A. Alan Carson, M.D.   B. The Andrew Carlton Nursing Home   1.____
   C. Prof., Alfred P. Carlton   D. Mr. A. Peter Carlton

2. A. Chas. A. Denner   B. H. Jeffrey Dener   2.____
   C. Charles Denner   D. Harold Dener

3. A. James C. Maziola   B. Joseph A. Mazzola   3.____
   C. James Maziola   D. J. Alfred Mazzola

4. A. Bureau of Family Affairs   B. Office of the Comptroller   4.____
   C. Department of Gas & Electricity   D. Board of Estimate

5. A. Robert Alan Pearson   B. John Charles Pierson   5.____
   C. Robert Allen Pearson   D. John Chester Pierson

6. A. The Johnson Manufacturing Co.   B. C.J. Johnston   6.____
   C. Bernard Johnsen   D. Prof. Corey Johnstone

7. A. Ninteenth Century Book Shop   B. Ninth Federal Bank   7.____
   C. 19th Hole Coffee Shop   D. 92nd St. Station

8. A. George S. McNeely   B. Hugh J. Macintosh   8.____
   C. Mr. G. Stephen McNeally   D. Mr. H. James Macintosh

KEY (CORRECT ANSWERS)

1. D 6. C
2. B 7. A
3. C 8. D
4. B
5. A

TEST 3

DIRECTIONS: Each of the following questions contains four names. For each question, choose the name that should be LAST if the four names are to be arranged in alphabetical order in accordance with the Rules for Alphabetical Filing given before. Read these rules carefully. Then, for each question, indicate in the space at the right the letter before the name that should be LAST in alphabetical order.

SAMPLE QUESTION
A. Jane Earl   (2)
B. James A. Earle (4)
C. James Earl   (1)
D. J. Earle   (3)

The numbers in parentheses show the proper alphabetical order in which these names should be filed. Since the name that should be filed LAST is James A. Earle, the answer to the Sample Question is B.

1. A. Steiner, Michael   B. Steinblau, Dr. Walter   1._____
    C. Steinet, Gary   D. Stein, Prof. Edward

2. A. The Paper Goods Warehouse B. T. Pane and Sons Inc.   2._____
    C. Paley, Wallace   D. Painting Supplies Inc.

3. A. D'Angelo, F.   B. De Nove, C.   3._____
    C. Daniels, Frank   D. Dovarre, Carl

4. A. Berene, Arnold   B. Berene, Arnold L.   4._____
    C. Beren, Arnold Lee   D. Berene, A.

5. A. Kallinski, Liza   B. Kalinsky, L.   5._____
    C. Kallinky, E.   D. Kallinsky, Elizabeth

6. A. Morgenom, Salvatore   B. Megan, J.   6._____
    C. J. Morgenthal Consultant Services D. Morgan, Janet

7. A. Ritter, G.   B. Ritter, George   7._____
    B. Riter, George H.   D. Ritter, G.H.

8. A. Wheeler, Adele N.   B. Wieler, Ada   8._____
    C. Weiler, Adelaide   D. Wheiler, Adele

9. A. Macan, Toby   B. Maccini, T.   9._____
    C. MacAvoy, Thomas   D. Mackel, Theodore

10. A. Loomus, Kenneth   B. Lomis Paper Supplies   10._____
    C. Loo, N.   D. Loomis Machine Repair Company

89

KEY (CORRECT ANSWERS)

1. C
2. A
3. D
4. B
5. D
6. C
7. B
8. B
9. D
10. A

TEST 4

DIRECTIONS: In the following questions there are five notations numbered 1 through 5 shown in Column I. Each notation is made up of a supplier's name, a contract number, and a date and is to be filed according to the following rules:

First: File in alphabetical order
Second: When two or more notations have the same supplier, file according to the contract number in numerical order beginning with the lowest number.
Third: When two or more notations have the same supplier and contract number, file according to the date beginning with the earliest date.

In Column II the numbers 1 through 5 are arranged in four ways to show different possible orders in which the merchandise information might be filed. Pick the answer (A, B, C, or D) in Column II in which the notations are arranged according to the above filing rules.

SAMPLE QUESTION

COLUMN I
1. Cluney   (4865)   6/17/72
2. Roster   (2466)   5/10/71
3. Altool   (7114)   10/15/72
4. Cluney   (5276)   12/18/71
5. Cluney   (4865)   4/8/72

COLUMN II
A. 2, 3, 4, 1, 5
B. 2, 5, 1, 3, 4
C. 3, 2, 1, 4, 5
D. 3, 5, 1, 4, 2

The correct way to file the notations is:
3. Altool   (7114)   10/15/72
5. Cluney   (4865)   4/8/72
1. Cluney   (4865)   6/17/72
4. Cluney   (5276)   12/18/71
2. Roster   (2466)   5/10/71

The correct filing order is shown by the numbers in front of each name (3, 5, 1, 4, 2). The answer to the Sample Question is the letter in Column II in front of the numbers 3, 5, 1, 4, 2. This answer is D.

COLUMN I
1. 1. Fenten   (38511) 1/4/73
   2. Meadowlane (5020)   11/1/72
   3. Whitehall   (36142) 6/22/72
   4. Clinton   (4141)   5/26/71
   5. Mester   (8006)   4/20/71

COLUMN II
A. 3, 5, 2, 1, 4
B. 4, 1, 2, 5, 3
C. 4, 2, 5, 3, 1
D. 5, 4, 3, 1, 2

2. 1. Harvard   (2286)   2/19/70
   2. Parker   (1781)   4/12/71
   3. Lenson   (9044)   6/6/72
   4. Brothers   (38380) 10/11/72
   5. Parker   (41400) 12/20/70

A. 2, 4, 3, 1, 5
B. 2, 1, 3, 4, 5
C. 4, 1, 3, 2, 5
D. 5, 2, 3, 1, 4

2 (#4)

		COLUMN I			COLUMN II	
3.	1.	Newtone	(3197)	8/22/70	A. 1, 4, 2, 5, 3	3.____
	2.	Merritt	(4071)	8/8/72	B. 4, 2, 1, 5, 3	
	3.	Writebest	(60666)	4/7/71	C. 4, 5, 2, 1, 3	
	4.	Maltons	(34380)	3/30/72	D. 5, 2, 4, 3, 1	
	5.	Merrit	(4071)	7/16/71		
4.	1.	Weinburt	(45514)	6/4/71	A. 4, 5, 2, 1, 3	4.____
	2.	Owntye	(35860)	10/3/71	B. 4, 2, 5, 3, 1	
	3.	Weinburt	(45514)	2/1/71	C. 4, 2, 5, 1, 3	
	4.	Fasttex	(7677)	11/10/71	D. 4, 5, 2, 3, 1	
	5.	Owntye	(4574)	7/17/71		
5.	1.	Premier	(1003)	7/29/70	A. 2, 1, 4, 3, 5	5.____
	2.	Phylson	(0031)	5/5/71	B. 3, 5, 4, 1, 2	
	3.	Lathen	(3328)	10/3/71	C. 4, 1, 2, 3, 5	
	4.	Harper	(8046)	8/18/72	D. 4, 3, 5, 2, 1	
	5.	Lathen	(3328)	12/1/72		
6.	1.	Repper	(46071)	10/14/72	A. 3, 2, 4, 5, 1	6.____
	2.	Destex	(77271)	8/27/72	B. 3, 4, 2, 5, 1	
	3.	Clawson	(30736)	7/28/71	C. 3, 4, 5, 2, 1	
	4.	Destex	(77271)	8/17/71	D. 3, 5, 4, 2, 1	
	5.	Destex	(77271)	4/14/71		

KEY (CORRECT ANSWERS)

1. B
2. C
3. C
4. A
5. D
6. C

1. C
2. A
3. C
4. D

2 (#5)

		COLUMN I			COLUMN II	
5.	1.	Abernathy	(712467)	6/23/20	A. 5, 3, 1, 2, 4	5.____
	2.	Acevedo	(680262)	6/23/18	B. 5, 4, 2, 3, 1	
	3.	Aaron	(967647)	1/17/19	C. 1, 3, 5, 2, 4	
	4.	Acevedo	(680622)	5/14/17	D. 2, 4, 1, 5, 3	
	5.	Aaron	(967647)	4/1/15		
6.	1.	Simon	(645219)	8/19/20	A. 4, 1, 2, 5, 3	6.____
	2.	Simon	(645219)	9/2/18	B. 4, 5, 2, 1, 3	
	3.	Simons	(645218)	7/7/20	C. 3, 5, 2, 1, 4	
	4.	Simms	(646439)	10/12/21	D. 5, 1, 2, 3, 4	
	5.	Simon	(645219)	10/16/17		
7.	1.	Rappaport	(312230)	6/11/21	A. 4, 3, 1, 2, 5	7.____
	2.	Rascio	(777510)	2/9/20	B. 4, 3, 1, 5, 2	
	3.	Rappaport	(312230)	7/3/17	C. 3, 4, 1, 5, 2	
	4.	Rapaport	(312330)	9/6/20	D. 5, 2, 4, 3, 1	
	5.	Rascio	(777501)	7/7/20		
8.	1.	Johnson	(843250)	6/8/17	A. 1, 3, 2, 4, 5	8.____
	2.	Johnson	(843205)	4/3/20	B. 1, 3, 2, 5, 4	
	3.	Johnson	(843205)	8/6/17	C. 3, 2, 1, 4, 5	
	4.	Johnson	(843602)	3/8/21	D. 3, 2, 1, 5, 4	
	5.	Johnson	(843602)	8/3/20		

KEY (CORRECT ANSWERS)

1.	C	5	A
2.	A	6.	B
3.	C	7.	B
4.	D	8.	D

TEST 6

DIRECTIONS: In each of the following questions there are four groups of names. One of the groups in each question is NOT in correct alphabetic order. Mark the letter of that group next to the number that corresponds to the number of the question.

1. A. Ace Advertising Agency; Acel, Erwin; Ad Graphics; Ade, E.J. & Co.
    B. Advertising Bureau, Inc.; Advertising Guild, Inc.; Advertising Ideas, Inc.; Advertising Sales Co.
    C. Allan Associates; Allen-Wayne, Inc.; Alley & Richards, Inc.; Allum, Ralph
    D. Anderson & Cairnes; Amos Parrish & Co.; Anderson Merrill Co.; Anderson, Milton

    1.____

2. A. Bach, Henry; Badillo, John; Baer, Budd; Bair, Albert
    B. Baker, Lynn; Bakers, Albert; Bailin, Henry; Bakers Franchise Corp.
    C. Bernhardt, Manfred; Bernstein, Jerome; Best, Frank; Benton Associates
    D. Brandford, Edward; Branstatter Associates; Brown, Martel; Browne, Bert

    2.____

3. A. Cone, Robert; Contempo, Bernard; Conti Advertising; Cooper, James
    B. Cramer, Zed; Creative Sales; Crofton, Ada; Cromwell, Samuel
    C. Cheever, Fred; Chernow Advertising; Chenault Associates; Chester, Arthur
    D. Chain Store Advertising; Chair Lawrence & Co.; Chaite, Alexander E.; Chase, Luis

    3.____

4. A. Delahanty, Francis; Dela McCarthy Associates; Delehanty, Kurnit; Delroy, Stewart
    B. Doerfler, B.R.; Doherty, Clifford; Dorchester Apartments; Dorchester, Monroe
    C. Drayer, Stella; Dreher, Norton; Dreyer, Harvey; Dryer, Lester
    D. Duble, Normal; Duevell, William C.; Du Fine, August; Dugan, Harold

    4.____

5. A. Esmond, Walter; Esty, Willia; Ettinger, Carl; Everett, Austin
    B. Enlos, Cartez; Entertainment, Inc.; Englemore, Irwin; Equity Associates
    C. Einhorn, Anna Mrs.; Einhorn, Arlene; Eisele, Mary; Eisele, Minnie Mrs.
    D. Eagen, Roy; Egale, George; Egan, Barrett; Eisen, Henry

    5.____

6. A. Funt, Rand Inc.; Furman, Fainer & Co.; Furman Roth & Co.; Fusco, Frank A.
    B. Friedan, Phillip; Friedman, Mitchell; Friend, Harvey; Friend, Herbert
    C. Folkart Greeting Cards; Food Service; Foote, Cornelius; Foreign Advertising
    D. Finkels, Eliot; Finnerman, John; Finneran, Joseph; Firestone, Albert

    6.____

7. A. Gubitz, Jay; Guild, Dorothy; Gumbiner, B.; Gussow, Leonard
    B. Gore, Smith; Gotham Art, Inc.; Gotham Editors Service; Gotham-Vladimir, Inc.
    C. Georgian, Wolf; Gerdts, H.J.; German News Co.; Germaine, Werner
    D. Gardner, Fred; Gardner, Roy; Garner, Roy; Gaynor & Ducal Inc.

    7.____

2 (#6)

8. A. Howard, E. T.; Howard, Francis; Howson, Allen; Hoyt, Charles
    B. Houston, Byron; House of Graphics; Rowland, Lynne; Hoyle, Mortimer
    C. Hi-Lite Art Service; Hickerson, J.M.; Hickey, Murphy; Hicks; Gilbert
    D. Hyman, Bram; Hyman, Charles B.; Hyman, Claire; Hyman, Claude

8._____

9. A. Idone, Leopold; Ingraham, Evelyn; Ianuzzi, Frank; Itkin, Simon
    B. Ideas, Inc.; Inter-Racial Press, Inc.; International Association; Iverson, Ford
    C. Il Trionofo; Inwood Bake Shop; Iridor, Rose; Italian Pastry
    D. Ionadi, Anthony Irena, Louise; Iris, Ysabella; Isabelle, Arlia

9._____

10. A. Jonas, Myron; Johnstone, John; Jones, Julius; Joptha, Meyer
    B. Jeanne's Beauty Shoppe; Jeger, Jans; Jem, H.; Jim's Grill
    C. Jacobs, Abraham & Co., Jacobs, Harold A.; Jacobs, Joseph; Jacobs, M.J.
    D. Japan Air Lines; Jensen, Arne; Judson, P.; Juliano, Jeremiah

10._____

KEY (CORRECT ANSWERS)

1.	D	6.	D
2.	B	7.	C
3.	C	8.	B
4.	A	9.	A
5.	B	10.	A

TEST 7

DIRECTIONS: Below are ten groups of names, numbered 1 through 10. For each group, three different filing arrangements of the names in the group are given. In only ONE of these arrangements are the names in correct filing order according to standard rules for filing. For each group, select the ONE arrangement, lettered A, B, C, that is CORRECT.

1.
   Arrangement A
   Nichols, C. Arnold
   Nichols, Bruce
   Nicholson, Arthur

   Arrangement B
   Nichols, Bruce
   Nichols, C. Arnold
   Nicholson, Arthur

   Arrangement C
   Nicholson, Arthur
   Nichols, Bruce
   Nichols, C. Arnold

   1.____

2.
   Arrangement A
   Schaefer's Drug Store
   Schaefer, Harry T.
   Schaefer Bros.

   Arrangement B
   Schaefer Bros.
   Schaefer, Harry T.
   Schaefer's Drug Store

   Arrangement C
   Schaefer Bros.
   Schaefer's Drug Store
   Schaefer, Harry T.

   2.____

3.
   Arrangement A
   Adams' Dime Store
   Adami, David
   Adams, Donald

   Arrangement B
   Adami, David
   Adams' Dime Store
   Adams, Donald

   Arrangement C
   Adami, David
   Adams. Donald
   Adams' Dime Store

   3.____

4.
   Arrangement A
   Newton, Jas. F.
   Newton, Janet
   Newton-Jarvis Law Firm

   Arrangement B
   Newton-Jarvis Law Firm
   Newton, Jas. F.
   Newton, Janet

   Arrangement C
   Newton, Janet
   Newton-Jarvis Law Firm
   Newton, Jas. F.

   4.____

5.
   Arrangement A
   Radford and Bigelow
   Radford Transfer Co.
   Radford-Smith, Albert

   Arrangement B
   Radford and Bigelow
   Radford-Smith, Albert
   Radford Transfer Co.

   Arrangement C
   Radford Transfer Co.
   Radford and Bigelow
   Radford-Smith, Albert

   5.____

6.
   Arrangement A
   Trent, Inc.
   Trent Farm Products
   20th Century Film Corp.

   Arrangement B
   20th Century Film Corp.
   Trent Farm Products
   Trent, Inc.

   Arrangement C
   Trent Farm Products
   Trent, Inc.
   20th Century Film Corp.

   6.____

7.
   Arrangement A
   Morrell, Ralph
   M.R.B. Paper Co.
   Mt. Ranier Hospital

   Arrangement B
   Morrell, Ralph
   Mt. Ranier Hospital
   M.R.B. Paper Co.

   Arrangement C
   M.R.B. Paper Co.
   Morrell, Ralph
   Mt. Ranier Hospital

   7.____

8.
   Arrangement A
   Vanity Faire Shop
   Van Loon, Charles
   The Williams Magazine Corp.

   Arrangement B
   The Williams Magazine Corp.
   Van Loon, Charles
   Vanity Faire Shop

   Arrangement C
   Van Loon, Charles
   Vanity Faire Shop

   8.____

9. Arrangement A
   Crane and Jones Ins. Co.
   Little Folks Shop
   L.J. Coughtry Mfg. Co.

   Arrangement B
   L.J. Coughtry Mfg. Co.
   Crane and Jones Ins. Co.
   Little Folks Shop

   Arrangement C
   Little Folks Shop
   L.J. Coughtry Mfg. Co.
   Crane and Jones Ins. Co.

   9._____

10. Arrangement A
    South Arlington Garage
    N.Y. State Dept. of Audit
       and Control
    State Antique Shop

    Arrangement B
    N.Y. State Dept. of Audit
       and Control
    South Arlington Garage
    State Antique Shop

    Arrangement C
    State Antique Shop
    South Arlington Garage
    N.Y. State Dept. of Audit
       and Control

    10._____

KEY (CORRECT ANSWERS)

1. B   6. C
2. C   7. A
3. B   8. A
4. A   9. B
5. B   10. B

TEST 8

DIRECTIONS: Below are ten groups of names, numbered 1 through 10. For each group, three different filing arrangements of the names in the group are given. In only ONE of these arrangements are the names in correct filing order according to standard rules for filing. For each group, select the ONE arrangement, lettered A, B, C, that is CORRECT.

1. Arrangement A
   Gillilan, William
   Gililane, Ethel
   Gillihane, Harry

   Arrangement B
   Gililane, Ethel
   Gillihane, Harry
   Gillilan, William

   Arrangement C
   Gillihane, Harry
   Gillilan, William
   Gililane, Ethel

   1.____

2. Arrangement A
   Stevens, J. Donald
   Stevenson, David
   Stevens, James

   Arrangement B
   Stevenson, David
   Stevens, J. Donald
   Stevens, James

   Arrangement C
   Stevens, J. Donald
   Stevens, James
   Stevenson, David

   2.____

3. Arrangement A
   Brooks, Arthur E.
   Brooks, H. Albert
   Brooks, H.T.

   Arrangement B
   Brooks, H.T.
   Brooks, H. Albert
   Brooks, Arthur E.

   Arrangement C
   Brooks, H. Albert
   Brooks, Arthur E.
   Brooks, H.T.

   3.____

4. Arrangement A
   Lafayette, Earl
   Le Grange, Wm. J.
   La Roux Haberdashery

   Arrangement B
   Le Grange, Wm. J.
   La Roux Haberdashery
   Lafayette, Earl

   Arrangement C
   Lafayette, Earl
   La Roux Haberdashery
   Le Grange, Wm. J.

   4.____

5. Arrangement A
   Mosher Bros.
   Mosher's Auto Repair
   Mosher, Dorothy

   Arrangement B
   Mosher's Auto Repair
   Mosher Bros.
   Mosher, Dorothy

   Arrangement C
   Mosher Bros.
   Mosher, Dorothy
   Mosher's Auto Repair

   5.____

6. Arrangement A
   Ainsworth, Inc.
   Ainsworth, George
   Air-O-Pad Co.

   Arrangement B
   Ainsworth, George
   Ainsworth, Inc.
   Air-O-Pad Co.

   Arrangement C
   Air-O-Pad Co.
   Ainsworth, George
   Ainsworth, Inc.

   6.____

7. Arrangement A
   Peters' Printing Co.
   Peerbridge, Alfred
   Peters, Paul

   Arrangement B
   Peterbridge, Alfred
   Peters, Paul
   Petters' Printing Co.

   Arrangement C
   Peters, Paul
   Peters' Printing Co.
   Peterbridge, Alfred

   7.____

8. Arrangement A
   Sprague-Miller, Elia
   Sprague (and) Reed
   Sprague Insurance Co.

   Arrangement B
   Sprague (and) Reed
   Sprague Insurance Co.
   Sprague-Miller, Ella

   Arrangement C
   Sprague Insurance Co.
   Sprague (and) Reed
   Sprague-Miller, Ella

   8.____

2 (#8)

9. Arrangement A
    Ellis, Chalmers Adv.
       Agency
    Ellis, Chas.
    Ellis, Charlotte

    Arrangement B
    Ellis, Chas.
    Ellis, Charlotte
    Ellis, Chalmers Adv.
       Agency

    Arrangement C
    Ellis, Charlotte
    Ellis, Chas.
    Ellis, Chalmers Adv.
       Agency

    9._____

10. Arrangement A
    Adams, Paul
    Five Acres Coffee Shop
    Fielding Adjust. Co.

    Arrangement B
    Five Acres Coffee Shop
    Adams, Paul
    Fielding Adjust. Co.

    Arrangement C
    Adams, Paul
    Fielding Adjust Co.
    Five Acres Coffee Shop

    10._____

KEY (CORRECT ANSWERS)

1.	B	6.	B
2.	C	7.	B
3.	A	8.	C
4.	C	9.	A
5.	B	10.	C

TEST 9

DIRECTIONS: Below in Section A is a diagram representing 40 divisional drawers in alphabetic file, numbered 1 through 40. Below in Section B is a list of 30 names to be filed, numbered 1 through 30, with a drawer number opposite each name, representing the drawer in which it is assumed a file clerk has filed the name.

Determine which are filed CORRECTLY and which are filed INCORRECTLY based on standard rules for indexing and filing. If the name is filed CORRECTLY, print in the space at the right the letter C. If the name is filed INCORRECTLY, print in the space at the right the letter I.

SECTION A

1 Aa-Al	6 Bs-Bz	11 Ea-Er	16 Gp-Gz	21 Kp-Kz	26 Mo-Mz	31 Qa-Qz	36 Ta-Ti
2 Am-Au	7 Ca-Ch	12 Es-Ez	17 Ha-Hz	22 La-Le	27 Na-Nz	32 Ra-Rz	37 Tj-Tz
3 Av-Az	8 Ci-Co	13 Fa-Fr	18 Ia-Iz	23 Lf-Lz	28 Oa-Oz	33 Sa-Si	38 U-V
4 Ba-Bi	9 Cp-Cz	14 Fa-Fz	19 Ja-Jz	24 Ma-Mi	29 Pa-Pr	34 Sj-St	39 Wa-Wz
5 Bj-Br	10 Da-Dz	15 Ga-Go	20 Ka-Ko	25 Mj-Mo	30 Ps-Pz	35 Su-Sz	40 X-Y-Z

SECTION B

	Name or Title	Drawer No.	
1.	William O'Dea	28	1.____
2.	J. Arthur Crawford	8	2.____
3.	DuPont Chemical Co.	10	3.____
4.	Arnold Bros. Mfg. Co.	2	4.____
5.	Dr. Charles Ellis	10	5.____
6.	Gray and Doyle Adv. Agency	16	6.____
7.	Tom's Smoke Shop	37	7.____
8.	Wm. E. Jarrett Motor Corp.	39	8.____
9.	Penn-York Air Service	29	9.____
10.	Corinne La Fleur	13	10.____
11.	Cartright, Incorporated	7	11.____

101

2 (#9)

12.	7th Ave. Market	24	12._____
13.	Ft. Schuyler Apts.	13	13._____
14.	Madame Louise	23	14._____
15.	Commerce Dept., U.S. Govt.	38	15._____
16.	Norman Bulwer-Lytton	6	16._____
17.	Hilton Memorial Library	17	17._____
18.	The Linen Chest Gift Shop	36	18._____
19.	Ready Mix Supply Co.	32	19._____
20.	City Service Taxi	8	20._____
21.	A.R.C. Transportation Co.	37	21._____
22.	New Jersey Insurance Co.	19	22._____
23.	Capt. Larry Keith	20	23._____
24.	Girl Scouts Council	15	24._____
25.	University of Michigan	24	25._____
26.	Sister Ursula	38	26._____
27.	Am. Legion Post #9	22	27._____
28.	Board of Hudson River Reg. Dist.	17	28._____
29.	Mid West Bus Lines	39	29._____
30.	South West Tours, Inc.	34	30._____

KEY (CORRECT ANSWERS)

1. C	11. C	21. I
2. I	12. I	22. I
3. C	13. C	23. C
4. C	14. I	24. C
5. I	15. C	25. I
6. C	16. C	26. I
7. C	17. C	27. I
8. I	18. I	28. C
9. C	19. C	29. I
10. I	20. C	30. C

TEST 10

DIRECTIONS: Each question or incomplete statement is followed by several suggested answers or completions. Select the one that BEST answers the question or completes the statement. *PRINT THE LETTER OF THE CORRECT ANSWER IN THE SPACE AT THE RIGHT.*

1. Of the following statements about the numeric system of filing, the one which is CORRECT is that it
   A. is the least accurate of all methods of filing
   B. eliminates the need for cross-referencing
   C. allows for very limited expansion
   D. requires a separate index

2. When more than one name or subject is involved in a piece of correspondence to be filed, the office assistant should GENERALLY
   A. prepare a cross-reference sheet
   B. establish a geographical filing system
   C. prepare out-guides
   D. establish a separate index card for noting such correspondence

3. A tickler file is MOST generally used for
   A. identification of material contained in a numeric file
   B. maintenance of a current listing of telephone numbers
   C. follow-up of matters requiring future attention
   D. control of records borrowed or otherwise removed from the file

4. In filing, the name Ms. "Ann Catalana-Moss" should GENERALLY be indexed as
   A. Moss, Catalana, Ann (Ms.)   B. Catalana-Moss, Ann (Ms.)
   C. Ann Catalana-Moss (Ms.)   D. Moss-Catalana, Ann (Ms.)

5. An office assistant has a set of four cards, each of which contains one of the following names.
   In alphabetic filing, the FIRST of the cards to be filed is
   A. (Ms.) Alma John
   B. Mrs. John (Patricia) Edwards
   C. John-Edward School Supplies, Inc.
   D. John H. Edwards

6. Generally, of the following, the name to be filed FIRST in an alphabetical filing system is
   A. Diane Maestro   B. Diana McElroy
   C. James Mackell   D. James McKell

7. According to generally recognized rules of filing in an alphabetic filing system, the one of the following names which normally should be filed LAST is
   A. Department of Education, New York State
   B. F. B. I.
   C. Police Department of New York City
   D. P.S. 81 of New York City

7.____

KEY (CORRECT ANSWERS)

1.	D	6.	C
2.	A	7.	B
3.	C		
4.	B		
5.	D		

FILING

EXAMINATION SECTION
TEST 1

DIRECTIONS: Questions 1 through 8 each show in Column I names written on four cards (lettered w, x, y, z) which have to be filed. You are to choose the option (lettered A, B, C, or D) in Column II which *BEST* represents the proper order of filing according to the Rules for Alphabetic Filing, given before, and the sample question given below. Print the letter of the correct answer in the space at the right.

SAMPLE QUESTION

Column I
w. Jane Earl
x. James A. Earle
y. James Earl
z. J. Earle

Column II
A. w, y, z, x
B. y, w, z, x
C. x, y, w, z
D. x, w, y, z

The correct way to file the cards is:
y. James Earl
w. Jane Earl
z. J. Earle
x. James A. Earle

The correct filing order is shown by the letters, y, w, z, x (in that sequence). Since, in Column II, B appears in front of the letters, y, w, z, x (in that sequence), B is the correct answer to the sample question.

Now answer the following questions using that same procedure.

		Column I		Column II	
1.	w.	James Rothschild	A.	x, z, w, y	1.____
	x.	Julius B. Rothchild	B.	x, w, z, y	
	y.	B. Rothstein	C.	z, y, w, x	
	z.	Brian Joel Rothenstein	D.	z, w, x, y	
2.	w.	George S. Wise	A.	w, y, z, x	2.____
	x.	S. G. Wise	B.	x, w, y, z	
	y.	Geo. Stuart Wise	C.	y, x, w, z	
	z.	Prof. Diana Wise	D.	z, w, y, x	
3.	w.	10th Street Bus Terminal	A.	x, z, w, y	3.____
	x.	Buckingham Travel Agency	B.	y, x, w, z	
	y.	The Buckingham Theater	C.	w, z, y, x	
	z.	Burt Tompkins Studio	D.	x, w, y, z	
4.	w.	National Council of American Importers	A.	w, y, x, z	4.____
	x.	National Chain Co. of Providence	B.	x, z, w, y	
	y.	National Council on Alcoholism	C.	z, x, w, y	
	z.	National Chain Co.	D.	z, x, y, w	

107

2 (#1)

5.   w.   Dr. Herbert Alvary   A.   w, y, x, z   5.____
      x.   Mr. Victor Alvarado   B.   z, w, x, y
      y.   Alvar Industries   C.   y, z, x, w
      z.   V. Alvarado   D.   w, z, x, y

6.   w.   Joan MacBride   A.   w, x, z, y   6.____
      x.   Wm. Mackey   B.   w, y, z, x
      y.   Roslyn McKenzie   C.   w, z, x, y
      z.   Winifred Mackey   D.   w, y, x, z

7.   w.   3 Way Trucking Co.   A.   y, x, z, w   7.____
      x.   3rd Street Bakery   B.   y, z, w, x
      y.   380 Realty Corp.   C.   x, y, z, w
      z.   Three Lions Pub   D.   x, y, w, z

8.   w.   Miss Rose Leonard   A.   z, w, x, y   8.____
      x.   Rev. Leonard Lucas   B.   w, z, y, x
      y.   Sylvia Leonard Linen Shop   C.   w, x, z, y
      z.   Rose S. Leonard   D.   z, w, y, x

KEY (CORRECT ANSWERS)

1. A
2. D
3. B
4. D
5. C
6. A
7. C
8. B

TEST 2

DIRECTIONS: Questions 1 through 7 each show in Column I four names (lettered w, x, y, z) which have to be entered in an agency telephone directory. You are to choose the option (lettered A, B, C, or D) in Column II which *BEST* represents the proper order for entering them according to the Rules for Alphabetic Filing, given before, and the sample question given below.

SAMPLE QUESTION

Column I
- w. Doris Jenkin
- x. Donald F. Jenkins
- y. Donald Jenkin
- z. D. Jenkins

Column II
- A. w, y, z, x
- B. y, w, z, x
- C. x, y, w, z
- D. x, w, y, z

The correct way to enter these names is:
- y. Donald Jenkin
- w. Doris Jenkin
- z. D. Jenkins
- x. Donald F. Jenkins

The correct order is shown by the letters y, w, z, x, in that sequence. Since, in Column II, B appears in front of the letters y, w, z, x, in that sequence, B is the correct answer to the sample question.

Now answer the following questions using the same procedure.

Column I / Column II

1.
- w. Lawrence Robertson
- x. Jack L. Robinson
- y. John Robinson
- z. William B. Roberson

   - A. x, y, w, z
   - B. w, z, x, y
   - C. z, w, x, y
   - D. z, w, y, x

2.
- w. P. N. Figueredo
- x. M. Alice Figueroa
- y. Jose Figueredo
- z. M. Alicia Figueroa

   - A. y, x, z, w
   - B. x, z, w, y
   - C. x, w, z, y
   - D. y, w, x, z

3.
- w. George Steven Keats
- x. George S. Keats
- y. G. Samuel Keats
- z. Dr. Samuel Keats

   - A. y, x, w, z
   - B. z, y, x, w
   - C. x, z, w, y
   - D. w, z, x, y

4.
- w. V. Merchant
- x. Dr. William Mercher
- y. Prof. Victor Merchant
- z. Dr. Walter Merchan

   - A. w, x, y, z
   - B. w, y, z, x
   - C. z, y, w, x
   - D. z, w, y, x

5.
- w. Brian McCoy
- x. William Coyne
- y. Mr. William MacCoyle
- z. Dr. D. V. Coyne

   - A. z, x, y, w
   - B. y, w, z, x
   - C. x, z, y, w
   - D. w, y, z, x

6.
- w. Ms. M. Rosie Buchanan
- x. Rosalyn M. Buchanan
- y. Rosie Maria Buchanan
- z. Rosa Marie Buchanan

A. z, y, x, w
B. w, z, x, y
C. w, z, y, x
D. z, x, y, w

6.____

7.
- w. Prof. Jonathan Praga
- x. Dr. Joan Prager
- y. Alan VanPrague
- z. Alexander Prague

A. w, z, y, x
B. w, x, z, y
C. x, w, z, y
D. x, w, y, z

7.____

KEY (CORRECT ANSWERS)

1. C
2. D
3. A
4. D
5. A
6. B
7. B

TEST 3

DIRECTIONS: Questions 1 through 10 each show in Column I names written on four cards (lettered w, x, y, z) which have to be filed. You are to choose the option (lettered A, B, C, or D) in Column II which *BEST* represents the proper order of filing according to the rules and sample question given below. The cards are to be filed according to the Rules for Alphabetical Filing, given before, and the sample question given below.

SAMPLE QUESTION

Column I
w. Jane Earl
x. James A. Earle
y. James Earl
z. J. Earle

Column II
A. w, y, z, x
B. y, w, z, x
C. x, y, w, z
D. x, w, y, z

The correct way to file the cards is:
y. James Earl
w. Jane Earl
z. J. Earle
x. James A. Earle

The correct filing order is shown by the letters y, w, z, x (in that order). Since, in Column II, B appears in front of the letters y, w, z, x (in that order), B is the correct answer to the sample question.

Now answer Questions 1 through 10 using the same procedure.

Column I

1.
w. John Smith
x. Joan Smythe
y. Gerald Schmidt
z. Gary Schmitt

Column II
A. w, x, y, z
B. y, z, x, w
C. y, z, w, x
D. z, y, w, x

2.
w. A. Black
x. Alan S. Black
y. Allan Black
z. Allen A. Black

A. w, x, y, z
B. w, y, x, z
C. w, y, z, x
D. x, w, y, z

3.
w. Samuel Haynes
x. Sam C. Haynes
y. David Haynes
z. Dave L. Haynes

A. w, x, y, z
B. x, w, z, y
C. y, z, w, x
D. z, y, x, w

4.
w. Lisa B. McNeil
x. Tom MacNeal
y. Lisa McNeil
z. Lorainne McNeal

A. x, y, w, z
B. x, z, y, w
C. y, w, z, x
D. z, x, y, w

5.
w. Larry Richardson
x. Leroy Richards
y. Larry S. Richards
z. Leroy C. Richards

A. w, y, x, z
B. y, x, z, w
C. y, z, x, w
D. x, w, z, y

111

6. w. Arlene Lane   A. w, z, y, x
    x. Arlene Cora Lane   B. w, z, x, y
    y. Arlene Clair Lane   C. y, x, z, w
    z. Arlene C. Lane   D. z, y, w, x

7. w. Betty Fish   A. w, x, z, y
    x. Prof. Ann Fish   B. x, w, y, z
    y. Norma Fisch   C. y, z, x, w
    z. Dr. Richard Fisch   D. z, y, w, x

8. w. Dr. Anthony David Lukak   A. w, y, z, x
    x. Mr. Steven Charles Lucas B. x, z, w, y
    y. Mr. Anthony J. Lukak   C. z, x, y, w
    z. Prof. Steven C. Lucas   D. z, x, w, y

9. w. Martha Y. Lind   A. w, y, z, x
    x. Mary Beth Linden   B. w, y, x, z
    y. Martha W. Lind   C. y, w, z, x
    z. Mary Bertha Linden   D. y, w, x, z

10. w. Prof. Harry Michael MacPhelps   A. w, z, x, y
    x. Mr. Horace M. MacPherson   B. w, y, z, x
    y. Mr. Harold M. McPhelps   C. z, x, w, y
    z. Prof. Henry Martin MacPherson   D. x, z, y, w

KEY (CORRECT ANSWERS)

1. C   6. A
2. A   7. C
3. D   8. D
4. B   9. C
5. B   10. A

TEST 4

DIRECTIONS: Answer Questions 1 through 5 on the basis of the following information:

A certain shop keeps an informational card file on all suppliers and merchandise. On each card is the supplier's name, the contract number for the merchandise he supplies, and a delivery date for the merchandise. In this filing system, the supplier's name is filed alphabetically, the contract number for the merchandise is filed numerically, and the delivery date is filed chronologically.

In Questions 1 through 5 there are five notations numbered 1 through 5 shown in Column I. Each notation is made up of a supplier's name, a contract number, and a date which is to be filed according to the following rules:

   First: File in alphabetical order;
   Second: When two or more notations have the same supplier, file according to the contract number in numerical order beginning with the lowest number;
   Third: When two or more notations have the same supplier and contract number, file according to the date beginning with the earliest date.

In Column II the numbers 1 through 5 are arranged in four ways to show four different orders in which the merchandise information might
be filed. Pick the answer (A., B, C, or D) in Column II in which the notations are arranged according to the above filing rules.

SAMPLE QUESTION

Column I	Column II
1. Cluney (4865) 6/17/02	A. 2, 3, 4, 1, 5
2. Roster (2466) 5/10/01	B. 2, 5, 1, 3, 4
3. Altool (7114) 10/15/02	C. 3, 2, 1, 4, 5
4. Cluney (5296) 12/18/01	D. 3, 5, 1, 4, 2
5. Cluney (4865) 4/8/02	

The correct way to file the cards is:
   3. Altool (7114) 10/15/02
   5. Cluney (4865) 4/8/02
   1. Cluney (4865) 6/17/02
   4. Cluney (5276) 12/18/01
   2. Roster (2466) 5/10/01

Since the correct filing order is 3, 5, 1, 4, 2, the answer to the sample question is D. Now answer Questions 1 through 5.

1.
Column I			Column II
1. warren	(96063)	3/30/03	A. 2, 4, 3, 5, 1
2. moore	(21237)	9/4/04	B. 2, 3, 5, 4, 1
3. newman	(10050)	12/12/03	C. 4, 5, 2, 3, 1
4. downs	(81251)	1/2/03	D. 4, 2, 3, 5, 1
5. oliver	(60145)	6/30/04	

1.____

2 (#4)

2. 1. Henry   (40552)   7/6/04   A. 5, 4, 3, 1, 2   2.____
    2. Boyd   (91251)   9/1/03   B. 2, 3, 4, 1, 5
    3. George   (8196)   12/12/03   C. 2, 4, 3, 1, 5
    4. George   (31096)   1/12/04   D. 5, 2, 3, 1, 4
    5. West   (6109)   8/9/03

3. 1. Salba   (4670)   9/7/03   A. 5, 3, 1, 2, 4   3.____
    2. Salba   (51219)   3/1/03   B. 3, 1, 2, 4, 5
    3. Crete   (81562)   7/1/04   C. 3, 5, 4, 2, 1
    4. Salba   (51219)   1/11/04   D. 5, 3, 4, 2, 1
    5. Texi   (31549)   1/25/03

4. 1. Crayone (87105)   6/10/04   A. 1, 2, 5, 3, 4   4.____
    2. Shamba   (49210)   1/5/03   B. 1, 5, 2, 3, 4
    3. Valiant (3152)   5/1/04   C. 1, 5, 3, 4, 2
    4. Valiant (3152)   1/9/04   D. 1, 5, 2, 4, 3
    5. Poro   (59613)   7/1/03

5. 1. Mackie   (42169)   12/20/03   A. 3, 2, 1, 5, 4   5.____
    2. Lebo   (5198)   9/12/02   B. 3, 2, 4, 5, 1
    3. Drummon (99631)   9/9/04   C. 3, 5, 2, 4, 1
    4. Lebo   (15311)   1/25/02   D. 3, 5, 4, 2, 1
    5. Harvin   (81765)   6/2/03

KEY (CORRECT ANSWERS)

1. D
2. B
3. B
4. D
5. C

1. B
2. A

2 (#5)

3. A. Ungerer   11/11/02 (537924)   A. 1, 5, 3, 2, 4   3.___
    B. Winters   1/10/02   (657834)   B. 5, 1, 3, 4, 2
    C. Ventura   12/1/02   (698694)   C. 3, 5, 1, 2, 4
    D. Winters   10/11/02 (675654)   D. 1, 5, 3, 4, 2
    E. Ungaro   1/10/02   (684325)

4. 1. Norton   3/12/03   (071605)   A. 1, 4, 2, 3, 5   4.___
    2. Morris   2/26/03   (068931)   B. 3, 5, 2, 4, 1
    3. Morse   5/12/03   (142358)   C. 2, 4, 3, 5, 1
    4. Morris   2/26/03   (068391)   D. 4, 2, 5, 3, 1
    5. Morse   2/26/03   (068391)

5. 1. Eger   4/19/02   (874129)   A. 3, 4, 1, 2, 5   5.___
    2. Eihler   5/19/03   (875329)   B. 1, 4, 5, 2, 3
    3. Ehrlich   11/19/02 (874839)   C. 4, 1, 3, 2, 5
    4. Eger   4/19/02   (876129)   D. 1, 4, 3, 5, 2
    5. Eihler   5/19/02   (874239)

6. 1. Johnson   12/21/02 (786814)   A. 2, 4, 3, 5, 1   6.___
    2. Johns   12/21/03 (801024)   B. 4, 2, 5, 3, 1
    3. Johnson   12/12/03 (762814)   C. 4, 5, 3, 1, 2
    4. Jackson   12/12/03 (862934)   D. 5, 3, 1, 2, 4
    5. Johnson   12/12/03 (762184)

7. 1. Fuller   7/12/02   (598310)   A. 2, 1, 5, 4, 3   7.___
    2. Fuller   7/2/02   (598301)   B. 1, 2, 4, 5, 3
    3. Fuller   7/22/02   (598410)   C. 1, 4, 5, 2, 3
    4. Fuller   7/17/03   (598710)   D. 2, 1, 3, 5, 4
    5. Fuller   7/17/03   (598701)

8. 1. Perrine   10/27/99 (637096)   A. 3, 4, 5, 1, 2   8.___
    2. Perrone   11/14/02 (767609)   B. 3, 2, 5, 4, 1
    3. Perrault 10/15/98 (629706)   C. 5, 3, 4, 1, 2
    4. Perrine   10/17/02 (373656)   D. 4, 5, 1, 2, 3
    5. Perine   10/17/01 (376356)

KEY (CORRECT ANSWERS)

1. B
2. A
3. B
4. D
5. D
6. B
7. D
8. C

TEST 6

DIRECTIONS: Each question or incomplete statement is followed by several suggested answers or completions. Select the one that *BEST* answers the question or completes the statement. *PRINT THE LETTER OF THE CORRECT ANSWER IN THE SPACE AT THE RIGHT.*

1. Which one of the following *BEST* describes the usual arrangement of a tickler file?   1.____

   A. Alphabetical   B. Chronological
   C. Numerical   D. Geographical

2. Which one of the following is the *LEAST* desirable filing practice?   2.____

   A. Using staples to keep papers together
   B. Filing all material without regard to date
   C. Keeping a record of all materials removed from the files
   D. Writing filing instructions on each paper prior to filing

3. The one of the following records which it would be *MOST* advisable to keep in alphabetical order is a   3.____

   A. continuous listing of phone messages, including time and caller, for your supervisor
   B. listing of individuals currently employed by your agency in a particular title
   C. record of purchases paid for by the petty cash fund
   D. dated record of employees who have borrowed material from the files in your office

4. Tickler systems are used in many legal offices for scheduling and calendar control. Of the following, the *LEAST* common use of a tickler system is to   4.____

   A. keep papers filed in such a way that they may easily be retrieved
   B. arrange for the appearance of witnesses when they will be needed
   C. remind lawyers when certain papers are due
   D. arrange for the gathering of certain types of evidence

5. A type of file which permits the operator to remain seated while the file can be moved backward and forward as required is *BEST* termed a   5.____

   A. lateral file   B. movable file
   C. reciprocating file   D. rotary file

6. In which of the following cases would it be *MOST* desirable to have two cards for one individual in a single alphabetic file? The individual has   6.____

   A. a hyphenated surname
   B. two middle names
   C. a first name with an unusual spelling
   D. a compound first name

KEY (CORRECT ANSWERS)

1. B
2. B
3. B
4. A
5. C
6. A

FILING
EXAMINATION SECTION
TEST 1

Questions 1-9.

DIRECTIONS: An important part of the duties of an office worker in a public agency is to file office records. Questions 1 through 9 are designed to determine whether you can file records correctly. Each of these questions consists of four names. For each question, select the one of the four names that should be FOURTH if the four names were arranged in alphabetical order. *PRINT THE LETTER OF THE CORRECT ANSWER IN THE SPACE AT THE RIGHT.*

1. A. 6th National Bank B. Sexton Lock Co. 1.____
   C. The 69th Street League D. Thomas Saxon Corp.

2. A. 4th Avenue Printing Co. B. The Four Corners Corp. 2.____
   C. Dr. Milton Fournet D. The Martin Fountaine Co.

3. A. Mr. Chas. Le Mond B. Model Express, Inc. 3.____
   C. Lenox Enterprises D. Mobile Supply Co.

4. A. Frank Waller Johnson B. Frank Walter Johnson 4.____
   C. Wilson Johnson D. Frank W. Johnson

5. A. Miss Anne M. Carlsen B. Mrs. Albert S. Carlson 5.____
   C. Mr. Alan Ross Carlsen D. Dr. Anthony Ash Carlson

6. A. Delaware Paper Co. B. William Del Ville 6.____
   C. Ralph A. Delmar D. Wm. K. Del Ville

7. A. The Lloyd Disney Co. B. Mrs. Raymond Norris 7.____
   C. Oklahoma Envelope, Inc. D. Miss Esther O'Neill

8. A. The Olympic Eraser Co. B. Mrs. Raymond Norris 8.____
   C. Oklahoma Envelope, Inc. D. Miss Esther O'Neill

9. A. Patricia MacNamara B. Eleanor McNally 9.____
   C. Robt. MacPherson, Jr. D. Helen McNair

Questions 10-21.

DIRECTIONS: Questions 10 through 21 are to be answered on the basis of the usual rules for alphabetical filing. For each question, indicate in the space at the right the letter preceding the name which should be THIRD in alphabetical order.

2 (#1)

10. A. Russell Cohen B. Henry Cohn 10.____
    C. Wesley Chambers D. Arthur Connors

11. A. Wanda Jenkins B. Pauline Jennings 11.____
    C. Leslie Jantzenberg D. Rudy Jensen

12. A. Arnold Wilson B. Carlton Willson 12.____
    C. Duncan Williamson D. Ezra Wilston

13. A. Joseph M. Buchman B. Gustave Bozzerman 13.____
    C. Constantino Brunelli D. Armando Buccino

14. A. Barbara Waverly B. Corinne Warterdam 14.____
    C. Dennis Waterman D. Harold Wartman

15. A. Jose Mejia B. Bernard Mendelsohn 15.____
    C. Antonio Mejias D. Richard Mazzitelli

16. A. Hesselberg, Norman J. B. Hesselman, Nathan B. 16.____
    C. Hazel, Robert S. D. Heintz, August J.

17. A. Oshins, Jerome B. Ohsie, Marjorie 17.____
    C. O'Shaugn, F.J. D. O'Shea, Frances

18. A. Petrie, Joshua A. B. Pendleton, Oscar 18.____
    C. Pertwee, Joshua D. Perkins, Warren G.

19. A. Morganstern, Alfred B. Morganstern, Albert 19.____
    C. Monroe, Mildred D. Modesti, Ernest

20. A. More, Stewart B. Moorhead, Jay 20.____
    C. Moore, Benjamin D. Moffat, Edith

21. A. Ramirez, Paul B. Revere, Pauline 21.____
    C. Ramos, Felix D. Ramazotti, Angelo

3 (#1)
KEY (CORRECT ANSWERS)

1.	C	11.	B
2.	A	12.	A
3.	B	13.	D
4.	B	14.	C
5.	D	15.	C
6.	A	16.	A
7.	C	17.	D
8.	D	18.	C
9.	B	19.	B
10.	B	20.	B

21. C

TEST 2

DIRECTIONS: Each question or incomplete statement is followed by several suggested answers or completions. Select the one that BEST answers the question or completes the statement. *PRINT THE LETTER OF THE CORRECT ANSWER IN THE SPACE AT THE RIGHT.*

Questions 1-4.

DIRECTIONS: Questions 1 through 4 are to be answered on the basis of the following alphabetical rules.

RULES FOR ALPHABETICAL FILING

Names of Individuals

The names of individuals are filed in strict alphabetical order, *first* according to the last name, *then* according to first name or initial, and *finally* according to middle name or initial. For example: George Allen precedes Edward Bell and Leonard Reston precedes Lucille Reston.

When last names are the same, for example, A. Green and Agnes Green, the one with the initial comes before the one with the name written out when the first initials are identical.

Prefixes such as De, O', Mac, Mc and Van are filed as written and are treated as part of the names to which they are connected. For example, Gladys McTeaque is filed before Frances Meadows.

1. If the following four names were put into an alphabetical list, what would the FIRST name on the list be?
   A. Wm. C. Paul
   B. W. Paul
   C. Alice Paul
   D. Alyce Paule

   1.____

2. If the following four names were put into an alphabetical list, what would the THIRD name on the list be?
   A. I. MacCarthy
   B. Irene MacKarthy
   C. Ida McCaren
   D. I.A. McCarthy

   2.____

3. If the following four names were put into an alphabetical list, what would the SECOND name on the list be?
   A. John Gilhooley
   B. Ramon Gonzalez
   C. Gerald Gilholy
   D. Samuel Gilvecchio

   3.____

4. If the following four names were put into an alphabetical list, what would the FOURTH name on the list be?
   A. Michael Edwinn
   B. James Edwards
   C. Mary Edwin
   D. Carlo Edwards

   4.____

Questions 5-9.

DIRECTIONS: Questions 5 through 9 consist of a group of names which are to be arranged in alphabetical order for filing.

5. Of the following, the name which should be filed FIRST is
   A. Joseph J. Meadeen
   B. Gerard L. Meader
   C. John F. Madcar
   D. Philip F. Malder

6. Of the following, the name which should be filed LAST is
   A. Stephen Fischer
   B. Benjamin Fitchmann
   C. Thomas Fishman
   D. Augustus S. Fisher

7. The name which should be filed SECOND is
   A. Yeatman, Frances
   B. Yeaton, C.S.
   C. Yeatman, R.M.
   D. Yeats, John

8. The name which should be filed THIRD is
   A. Hauser, Ann
   B. Hauptmann, Jane
   C. Hauster, Mary
   D. Rauprich, Julia

9. The name which should be filed SECOND is
   A. Flora McDougall
   B. Fred E. MacDowell
   C. Juanita Mendez
   D. James A. Madden

Questions 10-14.

DIRECTIONS: Questions 10 through 14 are to be answered based on an alphabetical arrangement of the following list of names.

Walker, Carol J.	Wacht, Michael	Wade, Ethel
Wall, Fredrick	Wall, Francis	Wall, Frank
Wachs, Paul	Walker, Carol L.	Wagner, Arthur
Walters, Daniel	Wade, Ellen	Wald, William
Wagner, Allen	Walters, David	Walker, Carmen

10. The 4th name on the alphabetized list would be
    A. Wade, Ellen
    B. Wade, Ethel
    C. Wagner, Allen
    D. Wagner, Arthur

11. The 7th name on the alphabetized list would be
    A. Walker, Carmen
    B. Walker, Carol J.
    C. Walker, Carol L.
    D. Wald, William

12. The name that would come immediately AFTER Wagner, Arthur on the alphabetized list would be
    A. Wade, Ethel
    B. Wagner, Allen
    C. Wald, William
    D. Walker, Carol L.

13. The name that would come immediately BEFORE Wall, Frank would be 13._____
    A. Wall, Francis   B. Wall, Fredrick
    C. Walters, David   D. Walters, Daniel

14. The 12th name on the alphabetized list would be 14._____
    A. Walker, Carol L.   B. Wald, William
    C. Wall, Francis   D. Wall, Frank

KEY (CORRECT ANSWERS)

1. C	6. B	11. D
2. C	7. C	12. C
3. A	8. A	13. A
4. A	9. D	14. D
5. C	10. B	

TEST 3

DIRECTIONS: Each question or incomplete statement is followed by several suggested answers or completions. Select the one that BEST answers the question or completes the statement. *PRINT THE LETTER OF THE CORRECT ANSWER IN THE SPACE AT THE RIGHT.*

Questions 1-8.

DIRECTIONS: Questions 1 through 8 are based on the Rules of Alphabetical Filing given below. Read these rules carefully before answering the questions.

Names of People

1. The names of people are filed in strict alphabetical order, first according to the last name, then according to first name or initial, and finally according to middle name or initial. For example: George Allen comes before Edward Bell, and Leonard P. Reston comes before Lucille B. Reston.

2. When last names are the same, for example, A. Green and Agnes Green, the one with the initial comes before the one with the name written out when the first initials are identical.

3. When first and last names are alike and the middle name is given, for example, John David Doe and John Devoe Doe, the names should be filed in alphabetical order of the middle names.

4. When first and last names are the same, a name without a middle initial comes before one with a middle name or initial. For example, John Doe comes before John A. Doe and John Alan Doe.

5. When first and last names are the same, a name with a middle initial comes before one with a middle name beginning with the same initial. For example, Jack R. Hertz comes before Jack Richard Hertz.

6. Prefixes such as De, O', Mac, Mc, and Van are filed as written and are treated as part of the names to which they are connected. For example, Robert O'Dea is filed before David Olsen.

7. Abbreviated names are treated as if they were spelled out. For example: Chas. is filed as Charles and Thos. is filed as Thomas.

8. Titles and designations such as Dr., Mr., and Prof. are disregarded in filing.

Names of Organizations

1. The names of business organizations are filed according to the order in which each word in the name appears. When an organization name bears the name of a person, it is filed according to the rules for filing names of people as given above. For example: William Smith Service Co. comes before Television Distributors, Inc.

2. Where bureau, board, office or department appears as the first part of the title of a governmental agency, that agency should be filed under the word in the title expressing the chief function of the agency. For example, Bureau of Budget would be filed as if written Budget, (Bureau of the). The Department of Personnel would be filed as if written Personnel, (Department of).

3. When the following words are part of an organization, they are disregarded: the, of, and.

4. When there are numbers in a name, they are treated as if they were spelled out. For example: 10th Street Bootery is filed as Tenth Street Bootery.

Each question from 1 through 8 contains four names numbered from 1 through 4 but not necessarily numbered in correct filing order. Answer each question by choosing the letter corresponding to the CORRECT filing order of the four names in accordance with the above rules.

SAMPLE QUESTION:
   I. Robert J. Smith
   II. R. Jeffrey Smith
   III. Dr. A. Smythe
   IV. Allen R. Smithers

   A. I, II, III, IV   B. III, I, II, IV   C. II, I, IV, III   D. III, II, I, IV

Since the correct filing order, in accordance with the above rules is II I, IV, III, the correct answer is C.

1.   I. J. Chester VanClief   II. John C. Van Clief
     III. J. VanCleve   IV. Mary L. Vance

    The CORRECT answer is:
     A. IV, III, I, II   B. IV, III, II, I   C. III, I, II, IV   D. III, IV, I, II

2.   I. Community Development Agency   II. Department of Social Services
     III. Board of Estimate   IV. Bureau of Gas and Electricity

    The CORRECT answer is:
     A. III, IV, I, II   B. 1, II, IV, III   C. II, I, III, IV   D. I, III, IV, II

3.   I. Dr. Chas. K. Dahlman   II. F. & A. Delivery Service
     III. Department of Water Supply   IV. Demano Men's Custom Tailors

    The CORRECT answer is:
     A. I, II, III, IV   B. I, IV, II, III   C. IV, I, II, III   D. IV, I, III, II

4. I. 48th Street Theater   II. Fourteenth Street Day Care Center
    III. Professor A. Cartwright   IV. Albert F. McCarthy

    The CORRECT answer is:
    A. IV, II, I, III   B. IV, III, I, II   C. III, II, I, IV   D. III, I, II, IV

5. I. Frances D'Arcy   II. Mario L. DelAmato
    III. William R. Diamond   IV. Robert J. DuBarry

    The CORRECT answer is:
    A. I, II, IV, III   B. II, I, III, IV   C. I, II, III, IV   D. II, I, III, IV

6. I. Evelyn H. D'Amelio   II. Jane R. Bailey
    III. Robert Bailey   IV. Frank Baily

    The CORRECT answer is:
    A. I, II, III, IV   B. I, III, II, IV   C. II, III, IV, I   D. III, II, IV, I

7. I. Department of Markets
    II. Bureau of Handicapped Children
    III. Housing Authority Administration Building
    IV. Board of Pharmacy

    The CORRECT answer is:
    A. II, I, III, IV   B. I, II, IV, III   C. I, II, III, IV   D. III, II, I, IV

8. I. William A. Shea Stadium   II. Rapid Speed Taxi Co.
    III. Harry Stampler's Rotisserie   III. Wilhelm Albert Shea

    The CORRECT answer is:
    A. II, III, IV, I   B. IV, I, III, II   C. II, IV, I, III   D. III, IV, I, II

Questions 9-18.

DIRECTIONS: Questions 9 through 18 each show in Column I names written on four ledger cards (lettered w, x, y, z) which have to be filed. You are to choose the option (lettered A, B, C, or D) in Column II which BEST represents the proper order for filing the cards.

SAMPLE

COLUMN I		COLUMN II	
w.	John Stevens	A.	w, y, z, x
x.	John D. Stevenson	B.	y, w, z, x
y.	Joan Stevens	C.	x, y, w, z
z.	J. Stevenson	D.	x, w, y, z

3 (#3)

The correct way to file the cards is:
y. Joan Stevens
w. John Stevens
z. J. Stevenson
x. John D. Stevenson

The correct order is shown by the letters y, w, z, x in that sequence. Since, in Column II, B appears in front of the letters y, w, z, x in that sequence, B is the correct answer to the sample question.

Now answer the following questions, using the same procedure.

9. COLUMN I
    w. Juan Montoya
    x. Manuel Montenegro
    y. Victor Matos
    z. Victoria Maltos

    COLUMN II
    A. y, z, x, w
    B. z, y, x, w
    C. z, y, w, x
    D. y, x, z, w

    9._____

10. COLUMN I
    w. Frank Carlson
    x. Robert Carlson
    y. George Carlson
    z. Frank Carlton

    COLUMN II
    A. z, x, w, y
    B. z, y, x, w
    C. w, y, z, x
    D. w, z, y, x

    10._____

11. COLUMN I
    w. Carmine Rivera
    x. Jose Rivera
    y. Frank River
    z. Joan Rivers

    COLUMN II
    A. y, w, x, z
    B. y, x, w, z
    C. w, x, y, z
    D. w, x, z, y

    11._____

12. COLUMN I
    w. Jerome Mathews
    x. Scott A. Matthew
    y. Charles B. Matthew
    z. Scott C. Mathewsw

    COLUMN II
    A. w, y, z, x
    B. z, y, x, w
    C. z, w, x, y
    D. w, z, y, x

    12._____

13. COLUMN I
    w. John McMahan
    x. John P. MacMahan
    y. Joseph DeMayo
    z. Joseph D. Mayo

    COLUMN II
    A. w, x, y, z
    B. y, x, z, w
    C. x, w, y, z
    D. y, x, w, z

    13._____

14. COLUMN I
    w. Raymond Martinez
    x. Ramon Martinez
    y. Prof. Ray Martinez
    z. Dr. Raymond Martin

    COLUMN II
    A. z, x, y, w
    B. z, y, x, w
    C. z, w, y, x
    D. y, x, w, z

    14._____

15. COLUMN I   COLUMN II   15.____
    w. Mr. Robert Vincent Mackintosh   A. y, x, z, w
    x. Robert Reginald Macintosh   B. x, w, z, y
    y. Roger V. McIntosh   C. x, w, y, z
    z. Robert R. Mackintosh   D. x, z, w, y

16. COLUMN I   COLUMN II   16.____
    w. Dr. D. V. Facsone   A. y, w, z, x
    x. Prof. David Fascone   B. w, y, x, z
    y. Donald Facsone   C. w, y, z, x
    z. Mrs. D. Fascone   D. z, w, x, y

17. COLUMN I   COLUMN II   17.____
    w. Johnathan Q. Addams   A. z, x, w, y
    x. John Quincy Adams   B. z, x, y, w
    y. J. Quincy Addams   C. y, w, x, z
    z. Jerimiah Adams   D. x, w, z, y

18. COLUMN I   COLUMN II   18.____
    w. Nehimiah Persoff   A. w, z, x, y
    x. Newton Pershing   B. x, z, y, w
    y. Newman Perring   C. y, x, w, z
    z. Nelson Persons   D. z, y, w, x

KEY (CORRECT ANSWERS)

1.	A	6.	D	11.	A	16.	C
2.	D	7.	D	12.	D	17.	B
3.	B	8.	C	13.	B	18.	C
4.	D	9.	B	14.	A		
5.	C	10.	C	15.	D		

TEST 4

Questions 1-13.

DIRECTIONS: Each question from 1 through 13 contains four names. For each question, choose the name that should be FIRST if he four names are to be arranged in alphabetical order in accordance with the Rule for Alphabetical Filing of Names of People given below. Read this rule carefully. Then, for each question, mark your answer space with the letter that is next to the name that should be first in alphabetical order.

<u>RULE FOR ALPHABETICAL FILING OF NAMES OF PEOPLE</u>

The names of people are filed in strict alphabetical order, first according to the last name, then according to the first name. For example; George Allen comes before Edward Bell, and Alice Reston comes before Lucille Reston.

<u>SAMPLE QUESTION</u>
A. Roger Smith (2)
B. Joan Smythe (4)
C. Alan Smith (1)
D. James Smithe (3)

The number in parentheses show the proper alphabetical order in which these names should be filed. Since the name that should be filed FIRST is Alan Smith, the correct answer to the sample question is C.

1. A. William Claremont B. Antonio Clements 1.____
   C. Anthony Clemente D. William Claymont

2. A. Wayne Fumando B. Sarah Femando 2.____
   C. Susan Fumando D. Wilson Femando

3. A. Wilbur Hanson B. Wm. Hansen 3.____
   C. Robert Hansen D. Thomas Hanson

4. A. George St. John B. Thomas Santos 4.____
   C. Frances Starks D. Mary S. Stranum

5. A. Franklin Carrol B. Timothy Carrol 5.____
   C. Timothy S. Carol D. Frank F. Carroll

6. A. Christie-Barry Storage B. John Christie-Barry 6.____
   C. The Christie-Barry Company D. Anne Christie-Barrie

7. A. Inter State Travel Co. A. Interstate Car Rental 7.____
   C. Inter State Trucking D. Interstate Lending Inst.

2 (#4)

8.   A. The Los Angeles Tile Co.   8.____
       B. Anita F. Los
       C. The Lost & Found Detective Agency
       D. Jason Los-Brio

9.   A. Prince Charles   B. Prince Charles Coiffures   9.____
       C. Chas. F. Prince   D. Thomas A. Charles

10.   A. U.S. Dept. of Agriculture   B. United States Aircraft Co.   10.____
       C. U.S. Air Transport, Inc.   D. The United Union

11.   A. Meyer's Art Shop   B. Frank B. Meyer   11.____
       C. Meyers' Paint Store   D. Meyer and Goldberg

12.   A. David Des Laurier   B. Des Moines Flower Shop   12.____
       C. Henry Desanto   D. Mary L. Desta

13.   A. Jeffrey Van Der Meer   B. Jeffrey M. Vander   13.____
       C. Jeffrey Van   D. Wallace Meer

KEY (CORRECT ANSWERS)

1.	A	6.	D	11.	A
2.	B	7.	B	12.	C
3.	C	8.	B	13.	D
4.	A	9.	D		
5.	C	10.	C		

TEST 5

Questions 1-10.

DIRECTIONS: Questions 1 through 10 are to be answered on the basis of the usual rules of filing. Column I lists, next to the numbers 1 to 10, the names of 10 clinic patients. Column II lists, next to the letters A to D, the headings of file drawers into which you are to place the records of these patients. For each question, indicate in the space at the right the letter preceding the heading of the file drawer in which the record should be filed.

COLUMN I	COLUMN II	
1. Charles Coughlin	A. Cab-Cep	1._____
2. Mary Carstairs	B. Ceq-Cho	2._____
3. Joseph Collin	C. Chr-Coj	3._____
4. Thomas Chelsey	D. Cok-Czy	4._____
5. Cedric Chalmers		5._____
6. Mae Clarke		6._____
7. Dora Copperhead		7._____
8. Arnold Cohn		8._____
9. Charlotte Crumboldt		9._____
10. Frances Celine		10._____

Questions 11-18.

DIRECTIONS: Questions 11 to 18 are to be answered on the basis of the usual rules of filing. Column I lists, next to the numbers 11 to 18, the names of 8 clinic patients. Column II lists, next to the letters A to O, the headings of file drawers into which you are to place the records of these patients. For each question, indicate in the space at the right the letter preceding the heading of the file drawer in which the record should be filed.

COLUMN I	COLUMN II	
11. Thomas Adams	A. Aab-Abi	11._____
	B. Abj-Ach	
12. Joseph Albert	C. Aci-Aco	12._____
	D. Acp-Ada	
13. Frank Anaster	E. Adb-Afr	13._____
	F. Afs-Ago	
14. Charles Abt	G. Agp-Ahz	14._____
	H. Aia-Ako	
15. John Alfred	I. Akp-Ald	15._____
	J. Ale-Amo	
16. Louis Aron	K. Amp-Aor	16._____
	L. Aos-Apr	
17. Francis Amos	M. Aps-Asi	17._____
	N. Asj-Ati	
18. William Adler	O. Atj-Awz	18._____

Questions 19-28.

DIRECTIONS: Questions 19 through 28 are to be answered on the basis of the usual rules of filing. Column I lists, next to the numbers 19 through 28, the names of 10 clinic patients. Column II lists, next to the letters A to D the headings of file drawers into which you are to place the medical records of these patients. For each question, indicate in the space at the right the letter preceding the heading of the file drawer in which the record should be filed.

COLUMN I	COLUMN II	
19. Frank Shea	A. Sab-Sej	19._____
20. Rose Seaborn	B. Sek-Sio	20._____
21. Samuel Smollin	C. Sip-Soo	21._____
22. Thomas Shur	D. Sop-Syz	22._____
23. Ben Schaefer		23._____
24. Shirley Strauss		24._____
25. Harry Spiro		25._____
26. Dora Skelly		26._____
27. Sylvia Smith		27._____
28. Arnold Selz		28._____

KEY (CORRECT ANSWERS)

1.	D	11.	D	21.	C
2.	A	12.	I	22.	B
3.	D	13.	K	23.	A
4.	B	14.	B	24.	D
5.	B	15.	J	25.	D
6.	C	16.	M	26.	C
7.	D	17.	J	27.	C
8.	C	18.	E	28.	B
9.	D	19.	B		
10.	A	20.	A		

www.ingramcontent.com/pod-product-compliance
Lightning Source LLC
Chambersburg PA
CBHW080736230426
43665CB00020B/2759